ABRAHAM LINCOLN WAS A BADASS:

Crazy But True Stories About
The United States' 16th President

BILL O'NEILL

ISBN: 978-1-64845-075-4

DON'T FORGET YOUR
FREE BOOKS

TABLE OF CONTENTS

Introduction 1

Chapter 1: Definitely Not a Privileged Life 5

Chapter 2: So Badass He Taught Himself............................10

Chapter 3: And in This Corner! 15

Chapter 4: The Black Hawk War...19

Chapter 5: A Tough Guy and a Family Man.........................24

Chapter 6: Not a Face for Politics 29

Chapter 7: Not Afraid to Take Controversial Stands 34

Chapter 8: Bad Enough to Rise Above Failure 40

Chapter 9: How Novel, An Honest Politician.......................44

Chapter 10: Blazing a Trail in the Courts................................48

Chapter 11: A House Divided' 53

Chapter 12: A Badass Orator..59

Chapter 13: The Father of the Republican Party....................64

Chapter 14: Embracing the Youth Vote...................................67

Chapter 15: Bad Enough to Defeat an Assassination Plot 71

Chapter 16: Just Like Caesar? 75

Chapter 17: Multiple Health Ailments Couldn't Stop
This Badass... 80

Chapter 18: Problems out West...84

Chapter 19: A True Badass Isn't Afraid to Fire a Few
People... 88

Chapter 20: The Low Point of Chancellorsville..................... 91

Chapter 21: Lincoln Was Also a Diplomat............................ 95

Chapter 22: Freeing the Slaves — Well, Some of the Them ... 99

Chapter 23: "Four Score and Seven Years Ago" 102

Chapter 24: Fighting the Copperheads.................................105

Chapter 25: "Let Us Not Judge, That Ye Be Not Judged" ..108

Chapter 26: Winning the War...111

Chapter 27: Mercy for the Vanquished?............................... 114

Chapter 28: The Father of a New America............................ 117

Chapter 29: Even a Badass Can't Stop an Assassin's
Bullets... 120

Chapter 30: One of the Most Badass Legacies of All
American Presidents 124

Conclusion 128

INTRODUCTION

Welcome to *Abraham Lincoln Was a Badass: Some Truly Amazing Stories about the United States' Sixteenth President*, a fun and engaging book that profiles one of America's most popular presidents, detailing just how much of a badass he really was. That's right; this book looks at President Lincoln's life from the perspective of how he used his mental, intellectual, and sometimes even physical toughness to become one of the country's most important presidents. This book follows Lincoln's life chronologically, focusing on ideas and events that made Honest Abe a true badass.

When you think about it, Lincoln's badass nature is a large part of why he remains so popular.

Starting with his early life, you'll read about how the kid who would become the Great Emancipator, wasn't born with a silver spoon. Unlike most other presidents, before *and* after him, Lincoln grew up poor and moved around a lot, learning valuable lessons along the way that would help him be successful later in life. Lincoln grew up on what was the frontier at the time, and he embodied the toughness and grittiness of the American spirit, which endeared him to voters. This spirit is also one of the reasons why he continues to be one of America's most popular presidents.

From an early age, as he grew up in the wilds of Kentucky and Indiana, Lincoln learned that physical fitness and toughness was important for good health. This view also proved to be indispensable in his later political career.

But Lincoln wasn't necessarily destined to be one of America's greatest politicians.

Abraham Lincoln was a true free spirit who - just like Thomas Jefferson, Andrew Jackson, and George Washington - encompassed and embraced America's badass nature. Lincoln was a self-taught and self-sufficient individual, who continually moved west following the march of the frontier. Along the way, Abe took some chances in business, some of which failed, worked the soil as a farmer, and even fought in an Indian war before settling down to become a lawyer and politician.

It would be an understatement to say that Lincoln wasn't an ordinary politician.

By the time Lincoln had decided to become a politician, he was already a full-fledged frontiersman and badass. He didn't grow up in a sheltered, privileged environment as most politicians do; at the time, even those on the frontier of Illinois were from relatively well-connected and privileged families. Therefore, Lincoln brought something new or possibly something old, to the political arena. At the very least, it was something that harkened back to the early years of America.

Yes, Lincoln was truly a self-made man, the type that personified the American spirit.

Although not considered to be a very good-looking man, Lincoln's tall frame was enough to intimidate plenty of his political opponents. It was when he spoke that his true political badassness became apparent to everyone. Lincoln enthralled his audiences with his plain yet often loquacious words when he gave speeches, and he dominated the stage when he took part in debates. If there is one thing that Lincoln excelled in more than any other president before him, and possibly all those after him, it was his speaking abilities.

Lincoln could write a speech that would make the toughest man cry and he could energize almost any crowd with what would normally be an ordinary address.

Abraham Lincoln's stature and speaking abilities may have helped guide him into the White House, but it was his decision-making abilities that cemented his reputation as one of America's most badass presidents.

As soon as Lincoln was elected, the country was thrust into the Civil War. The relatively young nation had already faced a couple of wars and crises before 1861 but nothing on the level of one half of the country taking up arms against the other. To many, it looked as if the American Union would be forever broken, and if someone else had been the president at the time, it very well may have turned out that way, but Abraham Lincoln was a badass who wouldn't let that happen.

Lincoln made some tough decisions during the war that weren't always popular and are criticized by many to this day, such as suspending *habeas corpus* and severely punishing rebellious Indians in Minnesota. However, like any true badass, he took full responsibility for his actions until the very end.

Keep reading to learn about just how much of a badass Abraham Lincoln was in 30 short stories that follow his life and times. At the end of every chapter, there are a set of related famous and memorable quotes said by Lincoln and a few other people affiliated with the sixteenth president.

So sit back, relax, and enjoy learning about just how much of a badass America's sixteenth president really was!

CHAPTER 1

DEFINITELY NOT A PRIVILEGED LIFE

There's an idea in many people's minds that most, if not all, American presidents were born into positions of privilege and power. The idea probably comes from the fact that throughout history, most leaders - no matter the country - have been part of a ruling, often oligarchic class. Additionally, many American presidents *did* come from wealth and power.

Washington and Jefferson were from "old money" plantation families in Virginia, and Kennedy was from a "new money" family in Massachusetts.

Scattered among the many privileged American presidents are plenty of self-made men from middle-class backgrounds, such as Jimmy Carter and Ronald Reagan. But if you had to identify one president who was the "anti-Washington" or "anti-Jefferson" in terms of family wealth, it would be none other than Abraham Lincoln.

Abraham Lincoln was born on February 12, 1809, to Thomas and Nancy Lincoln in rural Hardin County, Kentucky. Abraham spent the first five years of his life living in one-room cabins with his parents, older sister Sarah, and younger brother Thomas Junior.

Needless to say, Kentucky was quite a bit different back then.

It was on the edge of the frontier, with the local Indian tribes only recently having been driven from most of the state. Abraham's paternal grandfather died in an Indian raid in 1786. The Indian threat may have been eradicated from Kentucky when Abraham began his life, but the tough conditions of the frontier still existed. The family's homes were usually isolated, Abraham and Sarah didn't attend formal schooling, and Thomas Lincoln wasn't very good with his money.

While by all accounts Thomas Lincoln was a kind man and a talented carpenter, he made several bad investments in land and wasn't a very good farmer. Thomas' repeated failures ensured that the Lincoln family would constantly be on the move. In the process, young Abraham would learn some valuable lessons about life that would help shape him into the badass that he'd later become.

The School of Hard Knocks

Life on the American frontier was tough. The men and women who chose to build futures on the frontier had to be extremely self-reliant; there were no police, doctors, or government officials nearby if something went wrong. This environment of self-reliance was extremely conducive to young Abraham's upbringing—he learned the value of hard work and how precious and precarious life was.

Work wasn't something that young Abe particularly liked, as he preferred more intellectual pursuits, but he was far from lazy and always did his share of the work around the family farm. The work ethic he learned early in his life in Kentucky and Indiana no doubt contributed to his success as a lawyer and politician later in life.

He learned the second most important life lesson through a couple of particularly painful experiences.

The Lincoln's welcomed Thomas Junior to their family in 1812 or 1813, but he died just three days after his birth. It may sound cold, but Thomas Junior's death wasn't very noteworthy to the folks of rural Hardin County. Children frequently died on the frontier, and it was seen as fortuitous that Nancy didn't die as well.

Still, Abe was a sensitive soul, so the death of his younger brother lingered with him for his entire life.

But the Lincoln family didn't have time to grieve, especially since Thomas was busy losing the land he had purchased. The loss of land was partly due to the archaic way that Kentucky surveyed property lines at the time, and partly due to competition from slave-holding plantations. Thomas refused to buy slaves and was adamantly anti-slavery throughout his life, which he passed on to young Abe. Still, Thomas' refusal to buy slaves and the competition from slave-owning landowners was only a part of the reason for his business failures.

The primary reason was Thomas' poor business skills.

Thomas brought his family across the Ohio River to the free state of Indiana in 1816. The family homesteaded in southern

Indiana's Spencer County. Although the Lincoln's were still relatively poor and Abe and Sarah never attended formal schools, the family's finances were much better and things were more stable. Abe worked the family farm with his father, became literate by reading the Bible, and became well-known in the region for his axe throwing abilities - now that's badass!

But tragedy struck the Lincoln family once more on October 5, 1818, when Nancy died after drinking contaminated milk. The situation hit the Lincoln family hard in many ways. It was certainly a moral blow, as Abe was extremely close to his mother, but there were also practical implications of Nancy's death.

As mentioned earlier, the men *and* women of the American frontier had to be self-sufficient, tough, and real badasses. The women had to take care of all the domestic chores as well as help out with the animals and crops when needed. Because of this, Thomas left for Kentucky months after his wife died and returned with a new bride, Sally, in 1819. The couple proved to be a good pair and she was a supportive and loving stepmother to Abe.

Although Abraham Lincoln never forgot his mother, Sally had a profound impact on his life. Perhaps most important, Sally encouraged young Abe to learn, read, and explore the world. She saw the twinkle of genius in his eyes and did what she could to make it even brighter.

LINCOLN QUOTES ABOUT ETHICS, MORALS, AND CHARACTER

- "Character is like a tree and reputation its shadow. The shadow is what we think it is and the tree is the real thing."

- "No man has a good enough memory to be a successful liar."

- "I have always found that mercy bears richer fruits than strict justice."

- "It has been my experience that folks who have no vices have very few virtues."

- "And in the end, it's not the years in your life that count. It's the life in your years."

CHAPTER 2

SO BADASS HE TAUGHT HIMSELF

There were so many things that made Abraham Lincoln a badass. From the time he was born on the frontier until the day he died, Lincoln's life consisted of a series of badass events and him demonstrating his badass skills and knowledge, time after time. But perhaps the most badass thing about Abe's life, and one that's a bit overlooked, is the fact that he was an autodidact.

You're probably thinking: "An auto what?" Well, an autodidact is just a fancy way of saying someone is self-taught. Self-taught people are common and have had a profound effect on the world throughout history, but when it comes to American presidents, they are very rare.

Most American presidents have had some type of grade school level education, with many of the early presidents having been homeschooled by tutors, and nearly all attended colleges.

In more recent decades, nearly every president attended one of the elite universities in America.

But Abraham Lincoln was no ordinary American president.

Although Abraham Lincoln had little in terms of formal education, he was actually quite well-rounded compared to many. Lincoln was fairly well-read, while at the same time he was quite worldly, learning the skills of carpentry and farming at an early age. Lincoln also knew first-hand how tough life could be, which gave him an edge later in his political career, as it allowed him to connect with the voters and to be seen as someone truly capable of empathy.

There is little doubt, though, that an American president needs to have a considerable knowledge base, even in the mid-nineteenth century. Because Abe went out of his way to gain that knowledge, he truly is a badass.

A Thirst for Knowledge

As a child, Abraham Lincoln demonstrated a constant desire to learn about the world. Unlike today, where some form of school is mandatory for children, Abraham Lincoln grew up in a time when formal schooling was a luxury that many children simply didn't enjoy, especially those growing up on the frontier like Abe. Still, Abe's mother did what she could to get her children into rural farm schools in Kentucky.

After Abe's mother died and his stepmother Sally moved in to fill the role of mother, she also continued to make sure the Lincoln children knew how to read and write. Sally encouraged Abe's literacy, giving him, Sarah Lincoln, and her children from her first marriage lessons in the home. By the time Abe was fifteen, he probably only had about a year of formal education, but he possessed strong intellectual abilities.

Although not particularly religious, Abraham had a special ability to memorize and recite scripture. Lincoln's knowledge and utilization of scripture would later become a key part of his rise to power as he frequently cited verses in his speeches and debates.

He also displayed an undeniable charisma among his peers. Whenever young Abe talked, kids his age always listened. Abe was always able to draw crowds, whether he was reciting scripture or the lines from an original poem or story he wrote.

It was clear to Abe's stepmother and most of those who knew him that he wasn't cut out to be a farmer. It wasn't necessarily that he didn't have the skills to be a farmer, but his mind was other places while he worked. Abe's constant daydreaming led to conflicts with his father. Like many fathers of any era, Thomas Lincoln thought that his son should get his head out of the clouds and focus on practical pursuits.

Abe knew other things were in store for him in life, but he was just waiting for a sign.

The sign came in January 1828, when his sister died during childbirth. After Sarah died, Abe took all the knowledge he had acquired and went on the road, or the river in his case, to "find himself."

Abe's trip down the Ohio and Mississippi rivers to New Orleans was one of the most important lessons in his life. Young Lincoln learned about American geography, business, and politics all at the same time. He saw how the country was connected by the river routes, but he also saw how the nation was divided by slavery.

Needless to say, the education Lincoln received on the rivers was one he took with him to the White House.

In 1830, the Lincoln clan, which had grown quite large through marriage, moved from Indiana to Illinois. Abe was 21 at the time and not on the best of terms with his father. After helping the clan settle near Decatur, Abe struck out on his own in the small town of New Salem, Illinois.

Just like a true badass, Lincoln knew that he had to forge a path of his own in life—Abraham Lincoln was always a leader, never a follower.

Lincoln Quotes on Education and Knowledge

- "Books serve to show a man that those original thoughts of his aren't very new after all."

- "Upon the subject of education...I can only say that I view it as the most important subject which we as a people may be engaged in."

- "Human nature will not change. In any future great national trial, compared with the men of this, we shall have as weak and as strong, as silly and as wise, as bad and as good. Let us, therefore, study the incidents of this, as philosophy to learn wisdom from."

- "A capacity, and taste, for reading gives access to whatever has already been discovered by others."

- "The larger the island of knowledge the longer the shoreline of wonder. Wonder rather than doubt is the root of knowledge."

CHAPTER 3

AND IN THIS CORNER!

Many American presidents were quite athletic before attaining the highest office in the land, some playing basketball and football in college, while many have played tennis, golf, and jogged while in the White House. For the most part, physical fitness and the presidency go hand in hand. The president needs to project the image of a virile, healthy person, so staying fit is important.

And few could boast of Abraham Lincoln's physical fitness. It is also quite likely that few, if any, other presidents, even in their prime, could have beat Lincoln.

In addition to being a hands-on frontiersman, Abraham Lincoln was an accomplished wrestler.

His interest began when he moved to New Salem, Illinois. He worked as a merchant at a store and began wrestling in his spare time. The type of wrestling Lincoln did was known as "folk wrestling," which was directly derived from ancient Greek wrestling and influenced the wrestling that is undertaken in high schools and colleges today. Standing about 6'4, Lincoln didn't have the natural build of a wrestler—the best wrestlers tend to be short and stocky with a low center

15

mass - but his strength, intelligence, and conditioning carried him to a record of 300-1.

Yes, you read that right: Abraham Lincoln had a record of 300 wins and only one loss!

The record, which was meticulously researched by historians, was good enough to get Lincoln into the National Wrestling Hall of Fame in 1992. It was also good enough to help him launch his political career.

My President Can Beat Up Your President

As Lincoln traveled around Illinois whipping opponent after opponent, he built quite a name for himself in and out of the ring. After defeating one opponent, pumped up on adrenaline, Lincoln shouted to the crowd, "I'm the big buck of this lick. If any of you want to try it, come on and whet your horns!"

Now that's badass!

Lincoln even defeated New Salem's town bully, who was the leader of a gang called the Clary's Grove Boys. When he defeated the bully, Lincoln's grappling reputation continued to grow and followed him to the Blackhawk War in 1832.

While Lincoln was serving with a militia unit, word got around that the tall, lean enlisted man from New Salem was a legend in the ring. A match was set up between Lincoln and another badass recruit named Hank Thompson. Although Lincoln lost the match, he had already cemented his reputation as a true tough guy on the frontier.

Lincoln proved all he needed to in the wrestling ring by that point, so it was time for him to move on to bigger and better things. But the matches he wrestled would become legendary and would carry with him for the rest of his life.

All of Lincoln's future political opponents knew about his wrestling background, and you can almost be assured that they were at least a little bit intimidated by it.

LINCOLN QUOTES ON HEALTH AND SELF IMPROVEMENT

- "I am a slow walker, but I never walk back." – Abraham Lincoln

- "Boys, Abe Lincoln is the best fellow that ever broke into this settlement. He shall be one of us." – Jack Armstrong to his gang after being defeated by Lincoln.

- "Give me six hours to chop down a tree and I will spend the first four sharpening the axe." – Abraham Lincoln

- "Well, I wish some of you would tell me the brand of whiskey that Grant drinks. I would like to send a barrel of it to my other generals." – Abraham Lincoln

- "Rules of living: Don't worry, eat three square meals a day, say your prayers, be courteous to your creditors, keep your digestion good, steer clear of biliousness, exercise, go slow and go easy. May be there are other things that your special case requires to make you happy, but my friend, these, I reckon, will give you a good life." – Abraham Lincoln

CHAPTER 4

THE BLACK HAWK WAR

Although the last few American presidents have had little to no military experience, it was once practically an unwritten rule that a president had to have served in the military, preferably in a war. Some of the United States' most revered presidents led American troops in battle - George Washington, Theodore Roosevelt, and Dwight Eisenhower - while numerous others served as lower-level officers and privates, such as John F. Kennedy.

Yes, it was once an almost universal American idea that the president had to be physically and mentally tough. The way for the voters to know that was by looking at the candidate's war record.

So, what chance did Abraham Lincoln have to serve in a war?

Well, he was born too late for the American Revolution and was only three years old when the War of 1812 began. Lincoln was also obviously too old for the Civil War. He could've made the Mexican-American War if he were a career military man, but still would've been pushing 40 when that war broke out. By the time Lincoln hit his twenties, he wasn't thinking about a career in the military, although thoughts of the law and possibly politics were jumping around in his head.

However, in the 1830s, there were always wars to be fought in America; one only had to go to the frontier to find them.

It was the era of Manifest Destiny. Americans were constantly pushing westward and decimating the American Indians in the process. So if a young man wanted combat experience, he only had to sign up and it wouldn't be long before another Indian war was being fought.

And Illinois was still on the western frontier in the early 1830s.

On April 6, 1832, A Sauk Indian chief named Black Hawk decided to push back against Manifest Destiny when he led a force of several aligned Indian tribes across the Mississippi River from Iowa into northern Illinois. With that, the Black Hawk War had begun and Abraham Lincoln would get his chance to experience war, just as many other American presidents did before and after him.

Answering the Call to Arms

As a good patriotic American and a proud Illinoisan, Lincoln almost immediately joined a volunteer unit of the Illinois militia to go north and fight Black Hawk and his Indians. Despite having no military experience, Lincoln was elected captain of his company and given command.

It would be the first of many elections that Lincoln would win.

Lincoln may have dutifully signed up to risk his life on behalf of his state and country, but his tour of duty in the Black Hawk War was for the most part uneventful.

Abe and his men spent most of their time marching from one location to the next. Since most of the action in the war took place in northern Illinois and southern Wisconsin, and Lincoln's unit formed in central Illinois, a good deal of time was spent marching to the theater of war. Once Lincoln and his men arrived in the war zone, they usually missed battles by days or even hours.

The Black Hawk War ended in late August, but Lincoln had already been mustered out of the service on July 10, never having experienced combat.

But Lincoln's experience in the Black Hawk War wasn't a total bust.

Although he didn't see action, Abe did experience the horrors of war. His unit arrived after one particularly grisly battle, during which several militiamen from another unit had been killed and scalped by their Indian adversaries. Lincoln and his men had to bury the dead, which left a lasting impression on the future president. It was at that point that Abe realized that war wasn't a game, and when he later became the commander-in-chief, he tried to do whatever he could to avoid war with the South.

Lincoln also honed his leadership skills during the Black Hawk War.

Abe may not have been a true military man, but he was certainly a born leader. All of his men respected him for his forthrightness and honesty, which are traits that defined Lincoln throughout his life and political career. Lincoln also exhibited the 'it' factor that all true leaders have, a charisma that can't be manufactured or forced, despite his gangly - and what many considered unappealing - physical appearance.

Finally, Lincoln learned a good lesson in humility during the Black Hawk War.

As explained in the previous chapter, Honest Abe lost his only wrestling match during the Black Hawk War. The match took place after Lincoln's unit was initially mustered. To beat the boredom before they received their orders to march north, the company organized wrestling matches with another company. It was then that Lincoln lost his only wrestling match, but learned an important lesson in the process — there's always someone bigger who can take you down.

Lincoln was still a badass and could've beaten nearly all comers, but his youthful arrogance was tempered a bit. The Black Hawk War changed Lincoln and helped make him the man he would become.

Lincoln Quotes on Leadership

- "In this age, in this country, public sentiment is everything. With it, nothing can fail; against it, nothing can succeed. Whoever molds public sentiment goes deeper than he who enacts statutes, or pronounces judicial decisions."

- "I never had a policy; I have just tried to do my very best each and every day."

- "I believe that people should fight for what they believe and only what they believe."

- "Two principles have stood face-to-face from the beginning of time; and they will ever continue to struggle. The one is the common right of humanity and the other the divine right of kings."

- "If any man ceases to attack me, I never remember the past against him."

CHAPTER 5

A TOUGH GUY
AND A FAMILY MAN

By the time he was in his twenties, Abraham Lincoln was already a well-seasoned badass. He had for the most part educated himself, learned how to thrive on the frontier, and made a name for himself in the wrestling ring. He was undoubtedly a tough guy, a product of the frontier, and a true self-sufficient American.

But underneath Lincoln's rough and tough exterior was a sensitive soul who cared deeply about others, especially his family.

As mentioned earlier, Abe was deeply affected by the deaths of his brother, sister, and mother, and was extremely helpful and loyal to all of his family members. When the extended Lincoln family moved to Illinois, Abe continued to keep in contact with them and help out if needed, but he eventually also started a family of his own. As Lincoln worked as a merchant, lawyer, and politician, his wife and children were at his side.

And the love that Abraham Lincoln had for his family was far from phony.

Unlike many politicians today who use their families as props to get votes, Abraham Lincoln had a genuine affection for his wife and children and tried to keep them out of the spotlight as much as possible. Abe was always there for his family, and they were there with him when he breathed his last breath.

Unlucky in Love

When it came to women, Abraham Lincoln was no lady's man. Things just never seemed to work out for him, at least until he met his future wife Mary Todd in 1839 when he was 30. But before that time, he just couldn't seem to catch a break when it came to the opposite sex.

Lincoln was interested in women and finding a wife, but for a while, it seemed as though women just weren't interested in him. Maybe they found him physically unappealing, or maybe they thought that the frontier lawyer had no real future.

Obviously, they were all very, very wrong.

Lincoln's first major love interest was a woman named Ann Rutledge. The couple's relationship, which began in 1835, at first read like a fairy tale. Unfortunately, it ended as a tragedy. Ann was engaged to a questionable character that left New Salem in 1835 on business. The agreement was that once he returned, he'd marry Ann, but while he was away, Ann met and fell in love with Lincoln.

Abe and Ann kept their love for each other secret, although there's no evidence that anything "untoward" took place, and by all accounts, Lincoln was an absolute gentleman. If it weren't for Ann's engagement, the couple may have wed, but then tragedy struck.

Ann died of typhoid fever that year, leaving Lincoln depressed and alone.

Lincoln then arranged to marry a woman from Kentucky in 1836, but that relationship ended before it started. Abe refocused his energies on building up his law business and making a name for himself in central Illinois.

But the thought of starting a family was never far from Lincoln's mind.

Finally, as Lincoln began working as a lawyer in Springfield and making important contacts, he met and became engaged to Mary Todd in 1839. She was the daughter of a successful and influential lawyer in central Illinois.

The couple wed in 1842 but not before Abe had some serious doubts.

It was probably just normal wedding day jitters, though, as the couple went on to have four sons—Robert, Edward, Willie, and Tad. Edward died in 1850 and Willie died in the White House in 1862.

Yes, tragedy was never far from Abraham Lincoln's doorstep, but he certainly made the most of the time he had with his family. Although Abe's work as a lawyer and politician kept him away from home for long periods, he cherished the time he was able to spend with his wife and sons. Lincoln was said to spoil his sons and often let them have the run of the office he shared with his law partner, William Herndon.

Abe indulged some of his literary interests by reading poetry to Mary, he helped his boys with their studies, and he also made time to play games with them. Although Lincoln never considered himself a particularly religious man and even made statements against organized religion, he also took time to read the scriptures with his family.

Abraham Lincoln was a true tough guy and an intimidating foe to face in the courtroom or campaign trail, but in the safe confines of his home, he was a gentle giant.

LINCOLN QUOTES ON
FAITH AND FAMILY

- "All that I am or ever hope to be, I owe to my angel mother." – Abraham Lincoln

- "I have felt many and many a time that I wanted to wring their little necks, and yet out of respect for Lincoln I kept my mouth shut. Lincoln did not note what his children were doing or had done." – William Herndon on the misbehaviors of the Lincoln boys at the Lincoln-Herndon law office.

- "The more sects we have the better. They are all getting somebody in (to the Church) that the others could not: and even with the numerous divisions we are all doing tolerably well." – Abraham Lincoln

- "I am a patient man, always willing to forgive on the Christian terms of repentance; and also to give ample time for repentance." – Abraham Lincoln

- "The strength of a nation lies in the homes of its people." – Abraham Lincoln

CHAPTER 6

NOT A FACE FOR POLITICS

Since democracy became the standard for modern governments throughout the world, the standard has also been for leaders to be physically attractive. Of course, this isn't always the case, but more often than not, those who make it to the highest rungs of the political ladder tend to have the looks of the captain of the football team or the head cheerleader. This was generally true in Abraham Lincoln's time as well.

When Lincoln entered politics in the 1840s, a person's looks could even be used against him. Remember, this was long before the era of awareness about body image, so anything and everything was on the table to use against a political opponent, no matter how offensive, including their looks.

Political candidates were routinely attacked for being overweight, or underweight.

Political candidates were often targeted for not being handsome enough.

The ethnic backgrounds of political candidates were also often spuriously brought up during the particularly heated political environment of the 1850s.

For Abraham Lincoln, this meant that he had to be constantly on political defense on all three of these fronts. When Lincoln's political opponents weren't attacking him for being "pro-Black" or "anti-Southern," they were making fun of him for being too tall, too ugly, and possibly of mixed racial origins.

How much of any of that was a political liability for Lincoln can be debated, but there's no question that Lincoln broke the mold of a typical politician, both before or after him, which makes him a true trailblazer and a badass.

Unconventional Background and Looks

We've already established that Abraham Lincoln had a rather unpresidential background, at least conventionally speaking. The hard life Lincoln lived on the American frontier could have been a hindrance to his political success, and probably would have been for most men, but it ended up being a major part of the sixteenth president's success.

It would be difficult to imagine Lincoln becoming the president if he hadn't experienced living in a one-room cabin, teaching himself, farming on the frontier, and wrestling all comers.

But Abraham Lincoln also had to overcome his not-so-good looks.

At six feet four inches, Abraham Lincoln towered over most people of his time, but he was also quite lanky, reportedly weighing in between 180 and 190 pounds. Lincoln was naturally tan, had dark hair, and hazel eyes. His eyes rested deep in his head below his full, bushy eyebrows.

Perhaps Lincoln's unconventional looks can best be summarized by one of his contemporaries, Horace White a writer for the *Chicago Tribune*:

"At first glance, some thought him grotesque, even ugly, and almost all considered him homely. When preoccupied or in repose he certainly was far from handsome. At times he looked unutterably sad, as if every sorrow were his own, or he looked merely dull, with a vacant gaze."

When Lincoln rose through the political ranks, his opponents attempted to use his looks against him. Many newspapers printed caricatures of Lincoln, some showing him as a monkey or ape-man. Some opponents even suggested that due to his swarthy features, Lincoln was of mixed African or American Indian blood. Neither of those accusations was based on any facts, and despite such claims being potentially politically ruinous in the 1850s, they all bounced off honest Abe.

Lincoln knew that addressing such accusations was pointless; if he let them upset him, then he was only playing into his opponents; strategy. No, Lincoln took the calm, rational course and simply ignored any allegations about his looks and/or background. The only people who seemed to care about them didn't like him in the first place and weren't among his constituency.

In other words, he played it perfectly and didn't lose any votes.

Some people have suggested that Lincoln's particularly lanky features, especially his long hands and figures, points to him suffering from Marfan syndrome or an endocrine disorder. Although it will never be known for sure, it is interesting to consider and would be just another hurdle that Abraham Lincoln jumped over on his way to the presidency.

At first glance, it may seem as though Abraham Lincoln's background and looks worked against him, but a closer examination reveals just how intelligent and clever Lincoln was, as he turned those seemingly detrimental factors into positive attributes. When Abe began his ascent in Illinois politics, he helped craft a myth of his own along the way. Lincoln used his superb storytelling and speaking abilities to tell wide-eyed crowds about his humble origins and eventually learned how to use his unconventional looks to his advantage.

Lincoln never got angry when his opponents made fun of his appearance or made spurious claims, which demonstrated to the voters that he was a man who had self-control. He also learned to dress in a way that complimented his body type. Dark clothing went well with his hair and the stovetop hat Lincoln became so well known for made him look seven feet tall.

Abraham Lincoln knew that he couldn't change the way he looked, but he could do things to enhance the positive elements and mitigate the negative ones.

You have to admit, that was pretty badass for a politician in the 1850s!

LINCOLN QUOTES AND THINGS OUTSIDE YOUR CONTROL

- "I laugh because I must not cry, that is all, that is all."

- "The Lord prefers common-looking people. That is why he made so many of them."

- "Human nature will not change. In any future great national trial, compared with the men of this, we shall have as weak and as strong, as silly and as wise, as bad and as good. Let us, therefore, study the incidents of this, as philosophy to learn wisdom from."

- "The only difference between stepping stones and stumbling blocks is the way we address the rocks cast into our path."

- "We can complain because rose bushes have thorns, or rejoice because thorn bushes have roses."

CHAPTER 7

NOT AFRAID TO TAKE CONTROVERSIAL STANDS

One of the major disappointments that many people express about today's political system is the tendency for politicians to not stand for anything meaningful. American politicians of both major parties seem to blow with the winds, going whichever way seems to be the current of public opinion. It's true that the United States government is a democracy and therefore reliant upon public opinion to some degree, which Lincoln himself acknowledged, but it appears as though most contemporary politicians are simply empty vessels waiting to be filled with the opinions of their constituency - and ample contributions from some of their wealthier supporters.

This is not to say that these attitudes didn't exist in Lincoln's time, but honest Abe seemed to be much more – well - honest when it came to his opinions and political platforms.

As mentioned earlier, Lincoln was raised in an anti-slavery/free soil family, and he took those beliefs with him when he was first elected to the Illinois state House of Representatives in 1834 as a member of the Whig Party. And although Illinois entered the Union as a free state in 1818, it was far from a bastion of anti-slavery activity.

Still, Lincoln was always true to his beliefs no matter how much attention they attracted. He was one of only six representatives to vote against a resolution in the Illinois state assembly that recognized the right of slave states to practice slavery while condemning the work of abolitionists. Although this resolution was nonbinding, even in Illinois, which was a free state since it entered the Union, this stand placed Lincoln squarely in the anti-slavery camp at a time when it was clear that it would become *the* issue in the next few decades.

With that said, Lincoln was far from an abolitionist and was not a believer in racial equality - not really. Lincoln's often complex and sometimes seemingly contradictory views on race earned him more than a few enemies, yet he always came out ahead.

Lincoln the Free Soiler, Not Abolitionist

To better understand Lincoln's views on race and slavery, it's important to know that not everyone who was against slavery before the Civil War was necessarily in favor of racial equality. The Free Soil movement was against the spread of slavery into the Western territories because they believed it would hurt the small farmers who had come to comprise most of the Northwest (now the Midwest).

The Free Soil movement eventually became the Free Soil Party in the 1840s, which was based on the single issue of stopping the spread of slavery. Most of the people in the Free Soil movement were themselves small farmers and many were immigrants from Scandinavia and Germany.

By comparison, the abolitionist movement was much older, as old as the country itself. As the name states, it was a movement that aimed to abolish all slavery. Abolitionists tended to be more educated, from the middle and upper classes and were concentrated in urban areas of the Northeast. Many leading abolitionists were also women. Unlike the Free Soilers, most abolitionists did believe in racial equality.

Lincoln was a Free Soiler. He was a small farmer who, although having no hatred of the Black race, was also not an avowed egalitarian. Most of Lincoln's political constituents were also Free Soilers when it came to slavery, although he later allied with important abolitionists throughout the country.

In other words, when it came to race and slavery, things weren't always black and white; Abraham Lincoln often walked a fine line between different ideologies.

During the 1850s, when Lincoln became a national political figure, he became acquainted with members of the American Colonization Society (ACS). The ACS, like Lincoln, also held complex views on race and slavery. The ACS was very much anti-slavery, much like the abolitionists, but they didn't think Whites and Blacks should live in the same country. It dedicated most of its resources to freeing slaves and then sending them to other countries. The ACS was responsible for establishing the independent nation-state of Liberia in 1824.

By the time Lincoln became president, the ACS was attempting to establish new colonies for former slaves in parts of Haiti and what are now the nation-states of Belize and Panama. Lincoln also put forward a policy whereby former slaves would have limited rights in the country.

Needless to say, whichever stance Lincoln took on these controversial problems gained him new enemies. The colonization or "repatriation" policies earned him the ire of many abolitionists and influential former slaves, such as Frederick Douglass, while the idea of giving any rights to free slaves angered many Free Soilers and immigrants.

Lincoln knew that slavery and race were the biggest issues of his time, and would continue to be for generations, so he was willing to listen to all arguments. In the end, he took a stance on some issues that were unpopular with many.

It was that kind of fearlessness in the political arena that set Lincoln apart from his contemporaries and continues to do so among the countless forgettable politicians of today.

LINCOLN QUOTES ON
SLAVERY AND RACE

- "I would save the Union. I would save it the shortest way under the Constitution. The sooner the national authority can be restored; the nearer the Union will be "the Union as it was." If there be those who would not save the Union, unless they could at the same time save slavery, I do not agree with them. If there be those who would not save the Union unless they could at the same time destroy slavery, I do not agree with them. My paramount object in this struggle is to save the Union, and is not either to save or to destroy slavery. If I could save the Union without freeing any slave I would do it, and if I could save it by freeing all the slaves I would do it; and if I could save it by freeing some and leaving others alone I would also do that. What I do about slavery, and the colored race, I do because I believe it helps to save the Union; and what I forbear, I forbear because I do not believe it would help to save the Union." – August 22, 1862 letter from Abraham Lincoln to Horace Greeley of the *New York Tribune.*

- "You and we are different races. We have between us a broader difference than exists between almost any other two races. Whether it is right or wrong I need not discuss, but this physical difference is a great disadvantage to us both, as I think your race suffers very greatly, many of them, by living among us, while ours suffers from your presence. In a word, we suffer on each side. If this is admitted, it affords a reason at least why we should be separated." – Lincoln to a group of free Black ministers on August 14, 1862.

- "My first impulse would be to free all the slaves, and send them to Liberia, - to their own native land. But a moment's reflection would convince me that whatever of high hope (as I think there is) there may be in this, in the long run, its sudden execution is impossible." – Abraham Lincoln.

- "When you have succeeded in dehumanizing the Negro, when you have put him down, are you quite sure that the demon you have roused will not turn and rend you?" – Abraham Lincoln.

- "And inasmuch as they cannot so live, while they do remain together there must be the position of superior and inferior, and I as much as any other man am in favor of having the superior position assigned to the white race." – Abraham Lincoln in 1858 debate with Stephen Douglas.

CHAPTER 8

BAD ENOUGH TO RISE ABOVE FAILURE

One of the hallmarks of a true badass is his or her ability to rise above adversity and failure. Because badasses tend to be bigger risk-takers than the majority of the population, they also tend to face problems more frequently than most people as well. What separates the big dogs from the puppies, though, is how those problems are overcome - or if not overcome, used as a lesson. Overcoming adversity builds character, and all historical badasses had plenty of character.

A true badass knows how to take failures and incorporate them into his or her life to become part of future successes. Abraham Lincoln was able to do this on numerous occasions.

We've already seen how Lincoln's early life was no walk in the park, and as he entered into his early adulthood, things didn't necessarily get any easier. Abe had to try his hand at different professions before realizing that his true calling was in the law, and later in politics.

Finding Himself in New Salem

When Lincoln moved to New Salem, he never intended to be a politician. He also never planned to be a subsistence farmer like his father; rather, his plans were totally up in the air. After delivering loads of merchandise down the Mississippi River for a New Salem merchant named Denton Offutt, Lincoln eventually became a partner with him in his general store.

Abe worked the counter of the store, becoming a favorite among the locals, but the business failed. Maybe Lincoln just didn't have what it takes to be a businessman, but more likely, his mind was somewhere else.

As he met more and more people in the area, it was eventually suggested to him that he should run for the Illinois General Assembly/State House of Representatives. To those who knew Lincoln, and presumably to Lincoln himself, he seemed like a natural for politics: he was a good public speaker, was amiable, and had plenty of energy. So Abe threw his hat in the ring in 1832 but lost.

That made two significant professional failures in a relatively short period of time. Many would have let the situation discourage them, but Lincoln used both as a learning experience. From his business failure, he learned that he'd never be an entrepreneur, and from his political failure, he learned that he had to make connections.

Like every successful badass, Lincoln needed to have a few things break his way, yet at the same time; he had to put himself in a position to make his own luck. The Black Hawk War proved to be one such lucky break for Lincoln's political career in many ways. Lincoln avoided true combat but was able to make some important connections and hone his political skills during the war. When he returned to New Salem after the war, Abe embarked on a successful stint in the Illinois state House that lasted until 1842, working as a successful lawyer in central Illinois during that time.

Lincoln then ran for a US House seat in his congressional district in 1843 but lost in the Whig primary to John Hardin. This failure - if you could even call it a failure - proved to be only a minor setback.

By 1843, Abraham Lincoln was the new face of Illinois politics, and before too long, he became an unstoppable force.

LINCOLN QUOTES ON SUCCESS

- "Whatever you are, be a good one."

- "Nearly all men can stand adversity, but if you want to test a man's character, give him power."

- "I'm a success today because I had a friend who believed in me and I didn't have the heart to let him down."

- "There can be glory in failure and despair in success."

- "That some achieve great success, is proof to all that others can achieve it as well."

CHAPTER 9

HOW NOVEL, AN HONEST POLITICIAN

We truly live in cynical times. As an example of how cynical our world is today, it is commonly assumed in most countries that politicians are natural liars and that for many of them, if their mouth is open - then they're lying. If you look more deeply into it, often it's not so much that politicians are lying all the time but that they routinely make promises that they never keep and probably never intend to keep. Now that may not be lying in the strictest sense of the term, but it certainly isn't honest.

We've already discussed how Abraham Lincoln's honesty set him apart from many other politicians in American history, helping make him a legendary badass. Abe seemed to be honest in all of his business and personal dealings, and when he entered politics, he continued to be honest.

An honest politician! How was he successful?

If we think of honesty and success among politicians today, then there's no possible way that an honesty politician can be successful, at least not for very long. To understand this, you need to suspend your twenty-first-century cynicism for a little bit.

It was a different time in the mid-1800s. People respected politicians far more back then and in turn, politicians seemed to respect the people a bit more. And when a society has a higher level of trust, people tend to be more honest, even the politicians!

With that said, I think we can give Honest Abe even more credit. Yes, politicians probably were much more honest on average back then, but they weren't above lying and corruption. So the fact that Lincoln was never involved in a major scandal, nor did he tell the public lies, is deserving of discussion and is definitely pretty badass.

The 1846 Congressional Election

When Abe lost the Whig nomination for his district's congressional seat in 1843, he simply regrouped, made new contacts, and almost immediately began preparing for his next shot at the seat. Hardin served only one term and was succeeded by veteran Whig politician Edward Baker. Although Baker defeated Abe in the 1844 Whig Party primary, he did not run for a second term, resigning on Christmas Eve, 1846.

Lincoln ran in the general election for Illinois' 7th congressional district against Democrat Peter Cartwright. Although the district leant heavily toward the Whig Party and Lincoln was expected to win, it wasn't an open and shut case. The Mexican-American War had broken out in April 1846, becoming a campaign issue.

The war was initiated by Democrat President James Polk, and although it was largely seen by many as a pro-Democrat war and by some as a pro-slavery war, most Americans were willing to rally around the flag.

So being anti-war could have been a political liability.

But Lincoln had to set himself apart from his opponent, so he did take an anti-war stance. With that said, everything Lincoln wrote and stated publicly throughout his life indicates that he was genuinely anti-war, or at least he was never gung-ho about sending young men off to die in war.

He also took a strong stance against the westward expansion of slavery, which many believed would be the result of the Mexican-American War. Additionally and perhaps most important, Lincoln promised the voters of his district that he would only serve one term if elected.

Today, politicians routinely make similar promises, yet thirty, forty, even fifty years later; they still sit in the halls of Congress.

But Lincoln was a man of his word. After defeating Cartwright by more than 13% in the election, he went to Washington and got his first true taste of national politics. Although he was a bit of a fish out of the water, Lincoln made even more important contacts that he would utilize later for his White House run and during the Civil War. He considered taking a post as the territorial governor after Whig Zachary Taylor was elected president in 1848, but he decided that he'd had enough of the frontier at that point in his life.

Staying true to the promise that he made to the people of his district, honest Abe returned to Illinois to practice law at his Springfield office.

Lincoln knew that the future of America would be decided in the coming years, so he returned to prepare himself for his role in the major events that would grip the country.

Lincoln Quotes on Politics and Government

- "I know the American People are much attached to their government; I know they would suffer much for its sake; I know they would endure evils long and patiently, before they would ever think of exchanging it for another. Yet, notwithstanding all this, if the laws be continually despised and disregarded, if their rights to be secure in their persons and property, are held by no better tenure than the caprice of a mob, the alienation of their affections from the government is the natural consequence; and to that, sooner or later, it must come."

- "As to your proposals that a poll shall be opened in every precinct, and that the whole shall take place on the same day, I do not personally object."

- "Elections belong to the people. It's their decision. If they decide to turn their back on the fire and burn their behinds, then they will just have to sit on their blisters."

- "The ballot is stronger than the bullet."

- "The legitimate object of government is to do for a community of people whatever they need to have done, but can not do at all, or can not so well do, for themselves – in their separate, and individual capacities."

CHAPTER 10

BLAZING A TRAIL IN THE COURTS

Today, in most countries, if you want to become a lawyer, you have to apply to several law schools. If you do get accepted to one, chances are you'll have to go into a lifetime of debt just to pay for it. You'll study long hours for three years and hopefully graduate, after which you will then study for the bar in your state to become a licensed attorney. It's certainly enough to discourage many from entering the legal profession, but it didn't deter Abraham Lincoln from making a name for himself in courtrooms across Illinois.

And Lincoln was so badass he never took one class in law school!

Just as he was an autodidact in his early life, Abraham Lincoln taught himself the law. When he wasn't working at the general store in New Salem, Abe was reading up on all the statutes and acts pertaining to Illinois law. The hard work paid off, as Lincoln passed the bar exam the first time he took it in September 1836. By early 1837, Lincoln had moved to the booming city of Springfield, which was at the time, still two years from becoming the state capital.

But Lincoln always had a keen sense of history and the times he lived in, so he knew that it would soon become an important city.

Unlike lawyers today who specialize in one type of law, Lincoln took on clients in both civil and criminal cases and often argued the cases personally. Lincoln argued cases before the Illinois State Supreme Court 175 times, 51 of those as the sole counsel. Abe's legal career gave him more important contacts in the state of Illinois, but even more important were the public speaking skills he gained.

Abraham Lincoln truly had a badass legal career that would make any legal TV show today look boring by comparison.

Honest Abe

Some historians say that Abraham Lincoln earned his nickname "Honest Abe" through his lifetime of honest dealings with people in business, politics, and life generally; but others believe he got the moniker while he was a frontier lawyer. America may have been a different country back then, but the lawyer profession was very similar.

Similar to today, lawyers back then didn't always have the best reputations and the legal profession was viewed by many as being a bit shady. After all, people in legal trouble, who are often shady individuals, need lawyers, so lawyers are constantly rubbing elbows with the dregs of society.

But Abe didn't let them drag him down.

Instead, Abe rose above it all and earned quite a reputation for himself as an excellent lawyer and businessman, in terms of running profitable law practices. Lincoln's first law partner was a man named John T. Stuart. Stuart and Lincoln ran a successful office on 5th Street in Springfield for about four years before Stuart moved on to other ventures. Before he left, though, Stuart gave Lincoln many important contacts and helped him understand how the law could be a money-making business.

From 1841 to 1844, Lincoln was the junior partner in a law firm with Stephen Logan. As much as Lincoln learned the business end of lawyering from Stuart, he discovered the scope and complexity of the law working with Logan. After Logan left the business in 1844, Lincoln became the senior partner in a business with William Herndon.

Many of the cases Lincoln took were bankruptcies, often concerning the many railroads that were being cobwebbed across the country at the time.

But Abraham Lincoln's most memorable case truly cemented his reputation as a badass lawyer.

The case was an 1858 murder trial, in which William "Duff" Armstrong was accused of beating a man named James Metzker to death on August 27, 1857. If television was around at the time, this case surely would've been among those shown nonstop. It had everything: violence, a colorful cast, and a defense that seemed too good to be true.

The accused was the son of none other than Jack Armstrong, the former leader of the Clary's Grove Boys, whom Lincoln defeated in a wrestling match. It turns out the two men had mutual respect after the encounter, which later turned into a lifelong friendship. Jack had passed away just before his son was accused of murder, but his widow approached Lincoln for help.

Abe agreed to take the case *pro bono*.

The entire case rested upon the account of an eyewitness, who claimed to have seen the murder from 150 feet away in the middle of the night. Eyewitness testimony is tough to beat, especially when the eyewitness has no reason to lie. But Honest Abe had a trick up his long, slender sleeve.

Long before the internet was even a dream, people referred to a yearly publication known as the *Farmer's Almanac* for useful information. The *Almanac* published detailed information about economics, population, and weather, and in this case, Lincoln used the publication to show the court that the Moon was in the first quarter and low on the horizon.

In other words, at that time of night, it would have been nearly impossible for the witness to see anything from 150 feet away, never mind someone's face to make a positive ID.

It was the OJ Simpson courtroom moment of the time. Just as Simpson was unable to put the bloody glove used by the killer over his hands, Lincoln showed that the witness couldn't have possibly seen his client.

The evidence was enough for an acquittal.

Honest Abe could easily have gone on to become the greatest lawyer in Illinois' history. He could have been wealthier than he ever would be in government, but the pull of politics and public service kept tugging on his coattails.

Abraham Lincoln may have been a badass lawyer, but he had a greater destiny to fulfill.

LINCOLN QUOTES ON WORK

- "I could not sleep when I got on such a hunt for an idea until I had caught it; ...This was a kind of passion with me, and it has stuck by me; for I am never easy now, when I am handling a thought, till I have bounded it north, and bounded it south, and bounded it east, and bounded it west."

- "The hen is the wisest of all the animal creation, because she never cackles until the egg is laid."

- "Resolve to be honest at all events; and if in your own judgment you cannot be an honest lawyer, resolve to be honest without being a lawyer"

- "My father taught me to work, but not to love it. I never did like to work, and I don't deny it. I'd rather read, tell stories, crack jokes, talk, laugh -- anything but work."

- "The greatest fine art of the future will be the making of a comfortable living from a small piece of land."

CHAPTER 11

'A HOUSE DIVIDED'

We've looked at how turmoil and adversity can cause a person to rise above the problems and become even stronger. Honest Abe did this with the tough living conditions he was born with: learning how to survive on the frontier, teaching himself to read, and eventually teaching himself enough about the law to become a respected lawyer.

Yes, a true badass always finds a way to take advantage of the situation, no matter how difficult it may be. The scope of the situation a badass has to take advantage of varies with time and place. For most, it includes personal and economic barriers that need to be overcome, as Lincoln did in his early life, but sometimes there is the added pressure of everything taking place in a truly "historic moment."

In Abraham Lincoln's case, the "historic moment" that he had to deal with was the run-up to the Civil War. By 1850, it was becoming clear to most people that the US was on the road to war. The moderates from the North and South were being overshadowed and shouted down by abolitionists from the North and secessionists from the South. For most people, it wasn't necessarily a matter of *if* a civil war would come to America, but *when*.

When the 1850s began, Abraham Lincoln was an obscure political figure known only to the people of central Illinois, but in fewer than ten years, he was able to take advantage of the national political currents that were sweeping the nation to become the leader of the new Republican Party and eventually the President of the United States of America.

Lincoln's ascent from obscurity to the highest level in the land was meteoric, to say the least, which is another reason why the sixteenth president was such a badass!

A New Direction

As slavery became more and more of an issue going into the 1850s, the two major political parties of the era were woefully unprepared to deal with the tsunami of cultural and political changes that were on the political horizon.

The Compromise of the 1850s allowed Texas into the Union as a slave state, gave western territories the right to choose if they practiced slavery, and made the Fugitive Slave Act the law of the land. Later, the Kansas-Nebraska Act of 1854 organized those territories, giving the people the right to choose slavery or not. In Kansas, the situation became so turbulent that a mini-civil war erupted from 1854 to 1859 that became known as "Bleeding Kansas."

It was apparent to everyone in the country, including Abraham Lincoln, that the Whig Party was unable to take advantage of the wave of change overtaking the country. To Lincoln and other young, Free Soil Whigs, the future of the party should be anti-slavery. But, because the old guard of the Whigs didn't want to lose the support of Southern, slave-holding Whigs, the party only timidly opposed the *expansion* of slavery.

So, in what was perhaps the greatest shakeup in American political history, Lincoln and other young and upcoming Whigs left the party to start the Republican Party in 1854.

The survival of the Republican Party was never assured and many thought that it was doomed before it began. The early Republican Party was essentially a coalition of several different constituencies that had often competing goals.

There were the old school Whigs who realized that their old party was dead, and joined by them were younger Free Soil activists like Lincoln. Northern, urban abolitionists found a home in the early Republican Party, as did members of the anti-Catholic, anti-immigrant Know Nothing Party. Each of these groups tried to influence the party's platform, but when the Supreme Court made the momentous *Dred Scott* decision in 1857 that ruled slaves were not free in free territories, the Republican Party became the anti-slavery party.

And Abraham Lincoln was there to seize the political opportunity.

At that time, US senators were elected through their state assemblies, not by popular vote. In other words, in a year when a senate seat was up for election, whichever party won more state congressional districts selected the senator. In 1858, Democrat Senator Stephen A. Douglas was up for re-election. The still-new Republican Party had to choose a candidate, and Lincoln was able to wrangle the nomination quite easily.

After using his connections to gain the Republican Party's senate nomination, Lincoln gave one of his most badass speeches in Springfield on June 16, 1858. It was then that Lincoln uttered the famous words of his "House Divided" speech.

"A house divided against itself, cannot stand," it begins. "I believe this government cannot endure permanently half slave and half free."

Lincoln immediately caught the eye and imagination of the press, and then Americans from coast to coast. To many Southerners, he became the most hated man in America: a violent tyrant who was obsessed with ending the Southern way of life.

To many Northerners, he was an almost mythical hero: a paternalistic figure fighting for the rights of all Americans against the evil conspiracy of "slave power."

Lincoln knew that once he gave the "House Divided" speech, it was like letting a genie out of a bottle. Tensions between the factions were increased and the road to a possible war and/or secession appeared inevitable.

In the middle of all this turmoil, though, was Honest Abe with a calm hand. All of the years of his acquired experiences and knowledge, combined with his natural intelligence and leadership skills pushed him to the forefront of American political leadership at the time. Lincoln dominated on debate stages and from behind podiums to become the country's primary voice against slavery by 1858.

Lincoln Quotes About American History

- "As a nation, we began by declaring that 'all men are created equal.' We now practically read it 'all men are created equal, except negroes.' When the Know-Nothings get control, it will read 'all men are created equal, except negroes, and foreigners, and Catholics.' When it comes to this I should prefer emigrating to some country where they make no pretense of loving liberty – to Russia, for instance, where despotism can be taken pure, and without the base alloy of hypocrisy."

- "The new year of 1854 found slavery excluded from more than half the states by state constitutions and from most of the national territory by congressional prohibition. Four days later commenced the struggle which ended in repealing that congressional prohibition. This opened all the national territory to slavery and was the first point gained." – From Lincoln's "House Divided" speech.

- "The dogmas of the quiet past are inadequate to the stormy present. The occasion is piled high with difficulty and we must rise with the occasion. As our case is new, we must think anew and act anew. We must disenthrall ourselves, and then we shall save our country." – Lincoln's annual address to congress on December 1, 1862.

- "Let [the Constitution] be taught in schools, in seminaries, and in colleges, let it be written in primers, in spelling books and in almanacs, let it be preached from the pulpit, proclaimed in legislative halls, and enforced in courts of justice. And, in short, let it become the political religion of the nation."

- "This necessity had not been overlooked, but had been provided for, as well as might be, in the notable argument of "squatter sovereignty," other-wise called "sacred right of self-government," which latter phrase, though expressive of the only rightful basis of any government, was so perverted in this attempted use of it as to amount to just this: That if any one man choose to enslave another, no third man shall be allowed to object. That argument was incorporated into the Nebraska Bill itself, in the language which follows: It being the true intent and meaning of this act not to legislate slavery into an territory or state, nor to exclude it therefrom, but to leave the people there - of perfectly free to form and regulate their domestic institutions in their own way, subject only to the Constitution of the United States." – From Lincoln's "House Divided" speech.

CHAPTER 12

A BADASS ORATOR

Almost immediately after Lincoln gave his "House Divided" speech, the newspapers reported on it from coast to coast. The news stories spoke about the tall, lanky former-Whig congressman from Springfield, Illinois who was running for the US Senate in Illinois. Reporters noted that although not particularly good looking, Lincoln had an undeniable stage presence and a way with words that would make Shakespeare himself proud.

To the press, it seemed as though the nascent Republican Party had found its new rising star - and they had found grist that would help them sell copy.

But the pragmatic Lincoln knew that his "House Divided" speech wasn't even half the fight. Senator Douglas would be an incredibly difficult opponent to beat for numerous reasons. The Democrats held a majority in the Illinois House, and it was their votes that would decide the winner. Douglas was also a well-seasoned politician, an excellent public speaker in his own right, and perhaps most important, he was the incumbent.

So, Lincoln and the leaders of the Illinois Republican Party decided that their best chance of victory was bringing Abe to the people. They proposed to Douglas and the Democrats to have a series of seven debates in each of Illinois' congressional districts, from August 21 to October 15, 1858. These political events were the first of their kind in the United States and set the precedent for future political campaigns.

Crucially, through these debates, Abraham Lincoln was able to demonstrate his badass oratorical skills for the people of America.

The Lincoln-Douglas Debates

The seven debates between Lincoln and Douglas, which came to be known as the "Lincoln-Douglas Debates," concentrated primarily on the issue of slavery. By 1858, it was by far the biggest issue in the United States. Each man tried to paint the other into a political corner, but an examination of the transcripts shows that each was somewhat moderate in their position.

Douglas tried to portray Lincoln as a radical abolitionist and an advocate of racial equality. Lincoln responded that while he was against slavery, he didn't believe in racial mixing.

On the other hand, Lincoln depicted Douglas as a stooge for "slave power" in America and an unprincipled man. Douglas defended himself by arguing that he merely believed that each state should have the right to preserve slavery and that the new territories should be able to decide the issue based on the popular vote.

Things went back and forth between the two until the second debate in Freeport on August 27. Lincoln knew that he needed to score some major points if he had a chance of beating the senator, so Lincoln used a combination of his knowledge of the law, along with his sharp wit and speaking abilities, to paint Douglas into a rhetorical corner.

Lincoln argued that the recent *Dred Scott* decision could have theoretically brought slavery to a free state such as Illinois. When Douglas disagreed with Lincoln's legal assessment of the ruling, Lincoln asked Douglas how the theory of "popularity sovereignty," which was the idea that new territories could decide if they wanted slavery through the popular vote, and which was an idea that Douglas supported, could be squared with the decision.

Douglas wasn't ready for such a well-thought line of questioning. The senator responded that despite the court's ruling in *Dred Scott*, the citizens of the new territories could vote to prohibit slavery. It was about as moderate as one could get on the issue at the time, too moderate for Southern Democrats. To Southern Democrats, Douglas seemed weak and unreliable. But to Republicans across the North, Abraham Lincoln seemed like the perfect guy to lead them in the future.

For the voters of Illinois, though, the choice between the two men was as close as could be. Douglas won reelection by taking more districts, but Lincoln won the popular vote, showing that his and the Republican Party's popularity were growing. Lincoln and Douglas would square off again two years later, but in the meantime, Lincoln had a party to build.

LINCOLN QUOTES ON
SLAVERY AND POLITICS

- "The will of God prevails. In great contests each party claims to act in accordance with the will of God. Both may be, and one must be, wrong."

- "I hate [indifference to slavery] because of the monstrous injustice of slavery itself. I hate it because it deprives our republican example of its just influence in the world- enables the enemies of free institutions, with plausibility, to taunt us as hypocrites-causes the real friends of freedom to doubt our sincerity, and especially because it forces so many really good men amongst ourselves into an open war with the very fundamental principles of civil liberty-criticizing the Declaration of Independence, and insisting that there is no right principle of action but self-interest." – Abraham Lincoln at the August 21, 1858 Lincoln-Douglas debate in Ottawa, Illinois.

- "It is the eternal struggle between these two principles - right and wrong - throughout the world. They are the two principles that have stood face to face from the beginning of time; and will ever to struggle."

- "The next question propounded to me by Mr. Lincoln is, can the people of a territory in any lawful way, against the wishes of any citizen of the United States, exclude slavery from their limits prior to the formation of a state constitution? I answer emphatically, as Mr. Lincoln has heard me answer a hundred times from every stump in Illinois, that in my opinion the people of a territory can, by lawful means, exclude slavery from their limits prior to the formation of a state constitution." – Stephen Douglas on his "Freeport Doctrine" at the Lincoln-Douglass debate of August 27, 1858 in Freeport, Illinois.

- "I have never had a feeling politically that did not spring from the sentiments embodied in the Declaration of Independence."

CHAPTER 13

THE FATHER OF THE REPUBLICAN PARTY

Although Abe may have lost the senate seat to Douglas, it proved to be somewhat of a blessing in disguise. The Lincoln-Douglas debates were covered by newspaper reporters from around the country and the live events were attended by thousands. Before too long, everyone in the country, especially Republicans, knew who the lanky lawyer from Springfield was.

It didn't take long for the Republican Party to transform from an upstart third party to the "party of Lincoln." The Republican Party platform included limited policies of immigration, high tariffs, and most important, anti-slavery. The Republican Party was a new party that was going to tackle the most difficult and pervasive issue of the day, and to do so, it needed to be led by a relatively young and energetic man.

Who better to take the mantle than the former wrestler himself, Abraham Lincoln?

The major money people from all the factions within the Republican Party agreed that Lincoln would be the perfect face for their party and the man who could win them the

White House in 1860. Lincoln's frontier background would help him appeal to Midwest farmers, while his anti-slavery positions would win him the vote with abolitionists in the cities and Northeast. Republican leaders reasoned that they would get the Know Nothing vote without having to use overtly anti-immigrant rhetoric. They correctly reasoned that the former Known Nothings, often referred to as "nativists," would never vote for the Democrats, as they were viewed as the party of immigrants and Catholics.

They also knew that Lincoln's superb speaking abilities would get him even more votes, and his charisma would unite all the factions within the party.

When the Republican Party met for its convention in May 1860 in Chicago, veteran New York Senator William Seward was the immediate favorite. But as voting commenced, the different factions within the party let their dislike of Seward be known. Moderates believed Seward was too radical on the slavery issue, while former Know Nothings thought he was too accommodating on immigration.

Lincoln took advantage of the divisions within the party by making alliances and giving assurances, so that by the third round of voting, Honest Abe was the pick.

Once again, Abraham Lincoln seemingly came out of nowhere to win. He seemed to thrive on the challenge, as the more people underestimated him, the more impressive were his political victories.

Lincoln Quotes - Humorous

- "You can fool some of the people all of the time, and all of the people some of the time, but you cannot fool all of the people all of the time."

- "If I had another face, do you think I'd wear this one?"

- "If you call a dog's tail a leg, how many legs does it have?": "Four, because calling a tail a leg doesn't make it one."

- "When arguing with a fool, make sure the opponent isn't doing the exact same thing."

- "A drop of honey gathers more flies than a gallon of gall." – Although Lincoln did say this and made the proverb popular, it originated in Europe and was believed to have been first used in America by Benjamin Franklin.

CHAPTER 14

EMBRACING THE YOUTH VOTE

Today, in nearly every election cycle, there's always plenty of talk about capturing the "youth vote." What exactly constitutes the youth vote is never clearly stated, although most people believe it includes those aged 18 to 30. Traditionally in the United States, the Democrats have won the youth vote, yet getting young adults out to vote is another matter.

But it was Abraham Lincoln and the Republicans who were the first to seriously court the youth vote.

You have to remember that only men were allowed to vote at that time, and nearly all of the men who voted were White. Therefore, in an electorate that was overwhelmingly homogenous, the young men were a distinct demographic that could sway an election.

And in the late 1850s, young men in the North were very much pro-Republican. Some had come there from the Know Nothings, while others had genuine anti-slavery ideas, but all saw something new and fresh in Abraham Lincoln and the Republican Party.

Lincoln's charismatic speeches, which were printed widely throughout the country by the spring of 1860, became popular among politically-minded young men in the North. The slavery issue, combined with Lincoln's pro-labor views led many men to form an organization known as the "Wide Awakes." The Wide Awakes were decentralized, with chapters in every northern state and cities of all sizes, and very active. The Wide Awake members aimed to promote Republican candidates for office and to stand up to Democrat partisans, violently if needed.

It didn't take long for the Wide Awakes to resemble a paramilitary organization.

Members wore dark robes, glazed hats, and carried torches as they marched, sometimes several thousand strong. As ominous and intimating as the Wide Awakes may have looked - and violence often did accompany their marches - Lincoln made the cynical choice to support them.

Lincoln marched with the Wide Awakes in Harford, Connecticut in March 1860, and after he won the Republican nomination for the presidency, his campaign worked to bring the Wide Awakes more tightly into the Republican coalition. Once again, Lincoln proved what a badass politician he was; the ploy worked, with Abe easily winning the youth vote in the North.

Lincoln easily won the 1860 presidential election with 180 electoral votes, although he only won about 40% of the popular vote. The rest of the vote was split between North Democrat Stephen Douglas, Constitutional Union candidate John Bell, and Southern Democrat John Breckinridge.

Lincoln Quotes on History and Economics

- "Labor is prior to, and independent of, capital. Capital is only the fruit of labor, and could never have existed if labor had not first existed. Labor is the superior of capital, and deserves much the higher consideration."

- "Let every American, every lover of liberty, every well-wisher to his posterity, swear by the blood of the Revolution never to violate in the least particular the laws of the country, and never to tolerate their violation by others. As the patriots of seventy-six did to the support of the Declaration of Independence, so to the support of the Constitution and the Laws let every American pledge his life, his property, and his sacred honor; let every man remember that to violate the law is to trample on the blood of his father, and to tear the charter of his own and his children's liberty." – Abraham Lincoln address to the Young Men's Lyceum of Springfield, Illinois January 27, 1838.

- "His first item is, that the Rio Grande was the Western boundary of Louisiana, as we purchased it of France in 1803; and, seeming to expect this to be disputed, he argues over the amount of nearly a page to prove it true; at the end of which he lets us know, that by the treaty of 1819, we sold to Spain the whole country from the Rio Grande eastward, to the Sabine. Now, admitting, for the present, that the Rio Grande, was the boundary of

Louisiana, what, under heaven, had that to do with the *present* boundary between us and Mexico?" – Abraham Lincoln speech in the US Congress on January 12, 1848 about the conclusion of the Mexican-American War.

- "There has never been but one question in all civilization-how to keep a few men from saying to many men: You work and earn bread and we will eat it."

- "Fellow-citizens, we cannot escape history. We of this Congress and this Administration will be remembered in spite of ourselves. No personal significance or insignificance can spare one or another of us. The fiery trial through which we pass will light us down in honor or dishonor to the latest generation." – Abraham Lincoln from his address to Congress on December 1, 1862.

CHAPTER 15

BAD ENOUGH TO DEFEAT AN ASSASSINATION PLOT

By this point, it should be apparent that Abraham Lincoln was pretty much a badass in everything he did. He was a rough and rugged frontiersman who was self-taught on the law and life in general. He was physically tough yet a true family man, which all paved the way for him to become a success in the mentally tough world of politics.

Once Lincoln entered the political arena, he showed how tough he could be by rising above petty criticisms about his looks and giving all his opponents oratorical smack-downs.

Yes, Lincoln truly was a badass in just about everything he did, but sometimes the mark of a true badass, or at least a successful one, is knowing when discretion is the better part of valor.

After Lincoln won the election, he said his goodbyes to the people of Illinois and boarded a train in Springfield on February 11, 1861 to begin a nearly two-week, 70-city journey by train to Washington. Along the way, Lincoln addressed throngs of his supporters, but before arriving in Washington, he had to pass through the slave state of Maryland.

As the president got closer to his destination, word came to him of an assassination plot. Lincoln acted quickly and decisively, although some in the press accused him of being cowardly. In the end, just like any true badass, Lincoln didn't care what the press had to say—he had a country to run.

The Baltimore Plot

Things fell apart very quickly in the United States after Lincoln was elected. South Carolina seceded from the Union on December 10, 1861, and within two months was followed by Mississippi, Florida, Alabama, Georgia, Louisiana, and Texas. Those seven states would form the Confederate States of America on February 8, 1861, just days before Lincoln began his historic journey.

Lincoln still believed that there was a possibility that war could be avoided and that the wayward states could be re-grafted back into the Union. Or at least, that's what Lincoln publicly stated. The reality is that the two sides may as well have been separated by the Atlantic Ocean: and conflict was inevitable, and in early February, rumors were circulating that some were going to attempt to end it in one fell swoop.

It all came down to Maryland. Maryland was a slave state, had voted for Breckinridge, and was a hotbed of anti-Lincoln activity in early 1861. Tough talk about what people would like to do to Lincoln was commonly heard in the city's taverns.

But it was all talk: or was it? Allan Pinkerton, the founder of the famous Pinkerton Detective Agency, which would later become famous for chasing down outlaws in the Wild West, received a report from one of his agents that an attempt would be made on Lincoln's life when he passed through Baltimore, Maryland on February 23. The alleged plot involved several potential assassins armed with knives who would attack the president-elect when he walked through and greeted the crowd.

Lincoln was not immediately convinced of the report. Needless to say, presidential security was quite a bit different back then: there was no such thing as the Secret Service and Lincoln had only one bodyguard. A friend and confidant of Lincoln's, Ward Hill Lamon, suggested to Abe that he only needed to carry a pistol and Bowie knife for protection, and at first Lincoln seemed to agree.

But Pinkerton was an articulate and convincing man. By the time Lincoln arrived in Baltimore on February 23, he agreed to Pinkerton's plan. Pinkerton had his men cut all telegraph lines into Baltimore the night before to hinder communication between potential plotters. Then instead of making the stop in Baltimore, the train kept going to Washington.

Some pro-Democrat press outlets tried to make Lincoln look like a coward for not stopping in Baltimore, but most people in the North knew that it was probably a wise decision. True leaders have to make all types of decisions, including ones that may make them temporarily look bad.

And as we've already seen and will continue to see, Lincoln was the type of man who wasn't afraid to make tough decisions and was always willing to take responsibility for them.

Lincoln Quotes on Success

- "Always bear in mind that your own resolution to succeed is more important than any one thing." – Abraham Lincoln letter to Isham Reavis on November 5, 1855.

- "Towering genius distains a beaten path. It seeks regions hitherto unexplored." – Abraham Lincoln address to the Young Men's Lyceum of Springfield, Illinois on January 27, 1838.

- ". . . attach no consequence to the *place* you are in, or the *person* you are with; but get books, sit down anywhere, and go to reading for yourself." – Abraham Lincoln letter to William Grigsby on August 3, 1858.

- "The way for a young man to rise is to improve himself every way he can, never suspecting that anybody wishes to hinder him. Allow me to assure you that suspicion and jealousy never did help any man in any situation. There may sometimes be ungenerous attempts to keep a young man down; and they will succeed, too, if he allows his mind to be diverted from its true channel to brood over the attempted injury." – Abraham Lincoln letter to his business/law partner, William Herndon, on July 10, 1848.

- "In your temporary failure there is no evidence that you may not yet be a better scholar, and a more successful man in the great struggle of life, than many others, who have entered college more easily." – Abraham Lincoln letter to his oldest son Robert's friend George Latham, after Latham was rejected by Harvard.

CHAPTER 16

JUST LIKE CAESAR?

For just about every person who has ever won the US presidency, getting there was a dream come true that was accompanied by a "honeymoon" period during which the new president is given some time to settle into the new role. Of course, there are a few exceptions, but for nearly the first 100 years of America's history, that was the case.

Until Lincoln became president.

Lincoln's ascendency to the presidency set off a chain of events that many saw coming. As state after state seceded from the Union, it looked like there were few options on the table. Some say that Lincoln was naïve and didn't see things happening until it was too late, while others argue that Lincoln was an idealist who believed in the eternal good in man.

Abraham Lincoln thought that it was possible to talk the South out of the war.

And if there was anyone on Earth in 1861 who could have stopped the Civil War before it began using words alone, it would have been Abraham Lincoln. After all, Lincoln's loquacious words had a way of winning over his opponents and his charisma didn't hurt either.

But late 1861 - early 1862 was like no other time in the United States' history. Even if Lincoln promised the Southern states in writing that the government wouldn't interfere with slavery, the relationship had been permanently fractured.

The Northern and Southern States had grown apart for several decades and were effectively a married couple that was separated. When Lincoln was elected, the South decided it was going to sue for divorce.

Faced with this, Lincoln had to make some very serious decisions. They weren't decisions that he neither liked nor wanted to make, but they were decisions that had to be made. They were the type of decisions that separate an average, ordinary leader from a true badass. When all was said and done, Lincoln proved in his decision making that he truly was an American badass.

Suspending Habeas Corpus

When the Southern states began seceding from the Union, things moved very quickly. They established the Confederate States of America on February 8, 1861, with their first capital in Montgomery, Alabama. The war then began on April 12, 1861, when Confederate forces attacked Fort Sumter in South Carolina.

The Confederacy had crossed the Rubicon, so it was up to Lincoln to respond.

Lincoln made a few tactical errors at the beginning of the war. He underestimated the will of the Confederate forces, overestimated Union sentiment in the South, and overestimated the North's willingness to go to war.

Before the Confederate forces attacked Fort Sumter, a sizable minority in the North were fine with letting the Southern states secede, and as we've discussed throughout this book, most Northerners were anti-slavery but not necessarily for racial equality. Most Northerners didn't want slavery in their states, or for it to spread out West, but they were fine with it in the South.

And then there were those pesky border states.

By May 11, 1861, 11 states had formally seceded from the Union and joined the CSA. Kentucky and Missouri both send delegations to the CSA in late 1861 and had units that fought in the Confederacy, but both states officially stayed in the Union. Maryland and Delaware stayed in the Union but remained slave states.

So, needless to say, Lincoln had to navigate a confusing political mess in the first few months of the Civil War. We've already seen how Maryland had several pro-Confederate elements within it, which continued after war was declared. The leaders of Maryland decided to stay in the Union, but they also voted to close the rail lines.

Lincoln decided he had to move fast to nip the situation in the bud.

At the behest of General Winfield Scott, Lincoln had the military arrest a Democrat congressman from Maryland as well as the Baltimore's mayor, police chief, and entire city council and hold them without trial. He later also ordered pro-Confederate members of the Maryland state assembly to be arrested and held without trial.

This act was essentially an undeclared act of martial law and the suspension of *habeas corpus*, which guarantees Americans the right to bail, a speedy trial, and not to be held without charges.

It was certainly a badass, alpha move by the president and one that angered plenty of Northern Democrats. But once again, Lincoln showed his intelligence by knowing how far to take things. He only enacted martial law in limited places and released all of the prisoners within a few months.

Although some in Congress attacked Lincoln for suspending habeas corpus, the House and the Senate passed a bill in Mach 1863 that suspended it for the remainder of the war.

So, Lincoln was able to legally assume a Caesar-like role. Some would say that was pretty badass, while others would say it was tyrannical. I guess it depends on your perspective, right?

LINCOLN QUOTES ON POWER

- "Must a government be too strong for the liberties of its people or too weak to maintain its own existence?" – Abraham Lincoln's July 4, 1861 message to Congress.

- "The power confided in me will be used to hold, occupy and possess the property and places belonging to the government, and to collect the duties and imposts."

- "Do I not destroy my enemies when I make them my friends?"

- "I claim not to have controlled events, but confess plainly that events have controlled me."

- "Let every man remember that to violate the law is to trample on the blood of his father, and to tear the charter of his own and his children's liberty."

CHAPTER 17

MULTIPLE HEALTH AILMENTS COULDN'T STOP THIS BADASS

Aside from the many political and social battles that Abraham Lincoln fought throughout his lifetime, perhaps the biggest battle, or battles, he faced were health problems. Relatively speaking, when one considers the time and the limitations of medical science, Lincoln was pretty healthy for most of his life, but he was hit with some afflictions that would have put lesser men down. Some of those ailments emerged early in life, but some of the worst happened when he was the president.

One ongoing controversy is whether or not Abraham Lincoln was born with a genetic disease.

Since Lincoln's death, and with the advancement of medical technology, several scholars have proposed that he suffered from the disorder known as Marfan syndrome. Those afflicted with Marfan syndrome generally have abnormally large limbs, possibly like Lincoln, but they generally also suffer from cardiovascular problems and are often sterile - both very much not Lincolnesque.

Others have suggested that Lincoln suffered from multiple endocrine neoplasia type 2B (MEN2B), which is another genetic disorder whereby the afflicted tend to have elongated body features, similar to those seen in Marfan syndrome. The problem with this theory, though, is that most sufferers who have it die in their 30s.

No, Lincoln was more than likely just a tall, lanky guy. With that said, he did suffer from more than one serious health condition during his abbreviated life.

Most of the health problems Lincoln incurred when he was young were quite typical of the frontier in the early 1800s, although quite badass when you consider them. He was said to have been kicked in the head by a horse when he was a kid, suffered various other injuries while working on the family farm, and contracted malaria at least twice.

Remember, this was in the era before antibiotic medicine, so if you got sick, you had really did have to be tough otherwise you'd die.

The most serious illness Lincoln contracted was smallpox in November 1863. Although cowpox was often given as a vaccine to smallpox at the time, Lincoln had not taken it before a wave of the illness hit Washington in late 1863. It could have been devastating, as the Civil War was in its early stages and very much hanging in the balance.

If Lincoln had died, there's no telling what would have happened.

But Lincoln didn't just take to his bed with smallpox. Instead, he told very few people he had it and went about with his business of running the country during wartime. It may not have been the best thing to do for his health, and he may have spread the illness to some other people, but you have to admit that it was pretty badass!

How many world leaders can you think of that led their country in a war time, when they had smallpox or any major illness, for that matter?

LINCOLN QUOTES ON
HEALTH AND WELLNESS

- "I believe, if we take habitual drunkards as a class, their heads and their hearts will bear an advantageous comparison with those of any other class. There seems ever to have been a proneness in the brilliant and warm-blooded to fall into this vice." – Address by Lincoln to the Springfield Washington Temperance Society on February 22, 1842.

- "Whether or not the world would be vastly benefited by a total banishment from it of all intoxicating drinks seems not now an open question. Three-fourths of mankind confess the affirmative with their tongues, and I believe all the rest acknowledge it in their hearts."

- "The land, the earth God gave to man for his home ... should never be the possession of any man, corporation, (or) society ... any more than the air or water."

- "At 50, if you are on a diet on your birthday, you can't eat a piece of your birthday cake. So grab two, a piece in each hand and, lo and behold, you will be on a balanced diet! Happy birthday, old chum!"

- "I laugh because I must not cry, that is all, that is all."

CHAPTER 18

PROBLEMS OUT WEST

As we've already discussed, every badass leader in history had to make tough decisions that weren't always popular. Some of these decisions were questioned at the time, such as Lincoln's order to suspend habeas corpus in Maryland, but were later viewed as rational and strategically expedient.

But Lincoln also made one bold decision that was applauded by most people at the time, yet is today decried by many as one of his worst decisions.

As the Civil War was raging and it looked like the Confederacy could win, the Dakota Indians in southwestern Minnesota engaged American settlers and the army in a military conflict from August 17, 1862 to December 26, 1862, known as the Sioux Uprising or the U.S. Dakota War of 1862. The casualty count was 77 American soldiers dead, nearly 800 settlers killed, and more than 150 Sioux dead, 38 of them in the largest mass execution in American history.

The execution was originally intended to be 300 until President Lincoln commuted the sentences of all but 39 of them, with one getting a last-minute reprieve.

Some say that Lincoln's ordered public execution of the Dakota Indians was a stain on his legacy, while others point out that he was quite merciful considering the extremely difficult position that the uprising put him and the Union in, as it essentially opened another front in the Civil War.

The Dakota War of 1862

It is almost universally agreed that the culture clash between European explorers, later colonists, and settlers and the indigenous peoples of the Americas had terrible consequences for the latter group. After losing wars to the European and European descended governments, the Indians were often forced onto reservations where they would theoretically continue to live semi-autonomously.

But, of course, theory and reality are two different things.

When the US government claimed the Northwest Territory and settlers began trickling in, conflicts happened and treaties were signed between the government and the different tribes. The Dakota Indians of what would become the state of Minnesota signed a treaty that gave them semi-autonomy along a thin, 150-mile strip of the Upper Minnesota River.

It wasn't much, but the Dakota could hunt as they did before and were given allotments of food and other provisions by the government.

But then a combination of the Civil War as well as inept and/or greedy government agents cut off the agreed rations and an influx of settlers reduced the available wild game.

Exasperated by the situation, bands of Dakota struck out against military outposts and isolated settlers in the region. The Dakota raped and killed hundreds of settlers across southern Minnesota, many of them immigrants from Scandinavia and Germany, before the settlers fought back. Lincoln finally realized that the situation was on the verge of getting out of hand so he formed the Department of the Northwest on September 6, 1862 to assess the situation and eventually sent reinforcements.

With a force of nearly 2,000 men, US Army Colonel Henry Hastings Sibley, who was the governor at the time, defeated a slightly smaller Dakota force led by Chief Little Crow on the bluffs of southwestern Minnesota near Wood Lake.

Once the Battle of Wood Lake ended, the army spent the next three months capturing Dakota Indians. The tragic ending to the war was the execution of the 38 Dakota in Mankato, Minnesota. The survivors were then sent to reservations to live out their harsh lives.

Lincoln is today criticized for ordering the executions, but it is rarely pointed out that many in the Republican Party wanted him to execute even more.

It was truly one of the most difficult, yet least mentioned parts of Lincoln's presidency. Lincoln's actions during the Dakota War continue to be controversial, but few doubt that they were decisive and allowed him to refocus the military's efforts toward winning the Civil War.

Lincoln Quotes on the Military and Warfare

- "There's no honorable way to kill, no gentle way to destroy. There is nothing good in war. Except its ending."

- "Both parties deprecated war; but one of them would make war rather than let the nation survive; and the other would accept war rather than let it perish. And the war came." – Abraham Lincoln at his second inaugural address on March 4, 1865.

- "Honor to the soldier and sailor everywhere, who bravely bears his country's cause. Honor, also, to the citizen who cares for his brother in the field and serves, as he best can, the same cause."

- "If there is no military need for the building, leave it alone, neither putting anyone in or out of it, except on finding someone preaching or practicing treason, in which case lay hands on him, just as if he were doing the same thing in any other building."

- "Military glory-that attractive rainbow, that rises in showers of blood-that serpent's eye, that charms to destroy."

CHAPTER 19

A TRUE BADASS ISN'T AFRAID TO FIRE A FEW PEOPLE

We've seen how Lincoln had to make some pretty tough decisions throughout his life and once he became president, it was one tough decision after another. The first two years of the war were difficult for Lincoln, both on and off the battlefield. The Confederates defeated the Union Army in battle after battle, the Republicans lost their majority in the House of Representative, and Lincoln fought a bout of smallpox late in 1863.

It all would have brought down a lesser man, but Lincoln faced each problem head-on and kept moving forward. But if he hadn't done something about the mounting battlefield losses, he would not now be remembered as the epic badass that he is - he would have been the guy who lost the Union!

On paper, the Union should've won the war quickly and easily. The Union had a larger army, it was much better supplied by industrial cities in the North, and it had a near limitless supply of men who were coming to America from Ireland, Scandinavia, and the German-speaking kingdoms.

Yet, they kept losing battle after battle. The simple reality is that the Confederacy had better generals, at least early in the war.

Confederate General Robert E. Lee seemed to put fear into the heart of Union generals even when he was nowhere in the vicinity. Union generals were timid and afraid to engage the bright and crafty West Point graduate, and even when Lincoln personally ordered his generals to engage him, they rarely did.

So, just as any good executive would do, Lincoln fired his generals — again and again, and again.

Lincoln even fired General George McClellan twice before realizing that few of the men available could match Lee on the battlefield. Finally, Lincoln made Ulysses S. Grant Lieutenant-General of the Union Army on March 4, 1964. It proved to be the best wartime decision Lincoln made.

LINCOLN QUOTES ABOUT FRIENDSHIP AND LOYALTY

- "Stand with anybody that stands right, stand with him while he is right and part with him when he goes wrong."

- "Be with a leader when he is right, stay with him when he is still right, but, leave him when he is wrong."

- "I'm a success today because I had a friend who believed in me and I didn't have the heart to let him down."

- "We are not enemies, but friends. We must not be enemies. Though passion may have strained, it must not break our bonds of affection. The mystic chords of memory will swell when again touched, as surely they will be, by the better angels of our nature." – From Lincoln's first inaugural address on March 4, 1861.

- "If friendship is your weakest point then you are the strongest person in the world."

CHAPTER 20

THE LOW POINT OF CHANCELLORSVILLE

Make no mistake about it, before Grant there were a lot of inept generals leading the Union Army. Lincoln wasn't firing these men due to personality clashes. A true leader and a true badass always looks beyond petty disagreements and personal conflicts to reach a common goal and do what is right for the common good.

Abraham Lincoln was exactly that kind of man.

He knew that the Civil War was an existential battle for the survival of the country. It didn't matter what he thought of his generals, he was only concerned with results. And for there to be results, the Union generals needed to take bold, decisive action.

On the other side, the Confederacy took a much more proactive and bold strategy on the battlefield. Although they were literally outnumbered and outgunned, their morale was very high during the first two-plus years of the war. With this combined with their better commanders, they decided to take the fight to the Union by massing their forces in Virginia and making continual thrusts toward Maryland and the District of

Columbia. The Confederates never hoped to conquer the North, but instead wanted to force the Union to recognize their independence.

The Confederacy also hoped to get one or more of the European powers to recognize their independence.

The Confederacy's plan was simple - win enough battles that the average person in the North wouldn't want to keep fighting. It was so simple that by late 1863 it seemed all but assured.

By April 3, 1863, when the Union and Confederate armies met on the battlefield near Chancellorsville, Virginia, the two forces were moving in opposite directions—literally and figuratively. The Confederate Army, led by Lee, was charging north and seemed poised to take Washington, while the Northern army couldn't seem to get its bearings after a succession of ineffective generals was fired by Lincoln.

When the bloody battle ended on May 6, Lee had won yet another resounding victory and another Union general, this time Joseph Hooker, would be fired by Lincoln.

It can't be overstated how terrible Chancellorsville was for Lincoln and the Union when you put everything into perspective. The Confederate Army was on the move north, Union generals were woefully inferior compared to their Confederate counterparts, and the political will to fight the war was evaporating in the North.

But amid this haze of failure and negativity, and even after he contracted smallpox, Lincoln put on his stove-top hat and rallied the American people. He issued the Emancipation

Proclamation and appointed Grant as his top general, and before too long - the war had drastically changed course.

A lesser president probably would have given up after Chancellorsville.

LINCOLN QUOTES ABOUT LOSS, HOPE, AND OVERCOMING

- "My dream is of a place and a time where America will once again be seen as the last best hope of earth."

- "The loss of enemies does not compensate for the loss of friends."

- "The occasion is piled high with difficulty. We must rise to the occasion." – From Lincoln's December 1, 1862 address to Congress.

- "Adhere to your purpose and you will soon feel as well as you ever did. On the contrary, if you falter, and give up, you will lose the power of keeping any resolution, and will regret it all your life."

- "Surely God would not have created such a being as man, with an ability to grasp the infinite, to exist only for a day! No, no, man was made for immortality."

CHAPTER 21

LINCOLN WAS ALSO A DIPLOMAT

When most people think of the American Civil War, a purely domestic conflict usually comes to mind. After all, it was a war between two factions *within* the United States, over governance of the country and didn't involve diplomacy or foreign relations.

Or did it?

The Civil War was a bit more complex than most people think and there was some cloak and dagger and diplomacy taking place. President Lincoln was required not only to appoint the best generals who would bring him victory on the battlefield but also to navigate the tricky world of nineteenth-century foreign policy.

We know Abraham Lincoln was a badass frontiersman, public speaker, politician, and commander-in-chief, but a diplomatic incident that threatened to bring more countries into the Civil War, against the US, shows that he was also a badass in the diplomatic area.

The Trent Affair

Let's go back a bit to the early stages of the war. Things were still very much up in the air, the Confederates were winning their fair share of battles, and it looked as if Lincoln had no commander who could get the job done.

But there was one thing that Lincoln truly did command - the seas.

The Union Navy far outclassed anything the Confederacy had, and as the war progressed, the Union essentially blockaded the South in what became known as the "Anaconda Plan." The primary purpose of the Anaconda Plan was to keep the Confederacy from trading its valuable cotton with Europe. A secondary reason was to keep it from developing an alliance with anyone in Europe.

The Europeans may have been against slavery, but none of them wanted to see a united, strong America and the idea of developing a new trading partner was also a draw.

So, as the Union blockade ramped up, some interesting things were being captured off the shores of the South.

Like two Confederate diplomats named James Mason and John Slidell.

On November 8, 1861, the Union frigate *San Jacinto* pursued and captured the British mail packet *Trent* off the Bahamas islands, finding the Confederate envoys, and causing an international incident. It was an incident that Lincoln didn't want nor need at that point in the war.

There was immediate outrage in the North and many quarters of the government toward the British. To many, it seemed as though the country that the Americans had fought so hard to reject less than 100 years ago was back at it, trying to put them "back in their place." Many wanted blood and possibly even war with the British.

For their part, the British weren't particularly happy with their ship being captured, arguing that it was a violation of their sovereignty. Although slavery was by then very unpopular in Britain, many supported the Confederacy if only to "give it to the Yanks." Needless to say, Lincoln's options were limited, and whatever he chose to do would have major ramifications on the war.

As always, though, Lincoln listened to his inner voice, which was always the voice of reason. Lincoln eventually agreed to release Mason and Slidell from custody and continue on with their diplomatic mission to Britain. Some immediately saw it as a capitulation on Lincoln's part, but it was a well thought out move by Abe. British anti-American sentiment quickly evaporated and the Confederate push to receive international recognition was also severely dampened.

In the end, Lincoln knew that holding the Confederate diplomats could seriously hurt the Union cause but keeping them didn't help anything, so he decided to follow one of his favorite aphorisms: "A drop of honey gathers more flies than a gallon of gall."

LINCOLN QUOTES ABOUT DIPLOMACY, COMPROMISE, AND NEGOTIATING

- "Discourage litigation. Persuade your neighbors to compromise whenever you can."

- "We shall sooner have the fowl by hatching the egg than by smashing it." – From Abraham Lincoln's last speech on April 11, 1865.

- "I was losing interest in politics, when the repeal of the Missouri Compromise aroused me again. What I have done since then is pretty well known."

- "Don't criticize them; they are just what we would be under similar circumstances."

- "If you are going to fight, don't let them talk you into negotiating. But, if you are going to negotiate, don't let them talk you into fighting."

CHAPTER 22

FREEING THE SLAVES— WELL, SOME OF THE THEM

If you ask the average person what Abraham Lincoln is best known for, a majority will probably tell you "he freed the slaves." Although this is true in the big picture - since the Civil War ultimately did lead to the end of slavery in the United States - it is only partially true.

Yes, Lincoln was against slavery, but he was more in favor of preserving the Union, and he said on numerous occasions that if he could preserve the Union and keep slavery, he would. If you're reading this and already know a little bit about the Civil War and the sixteenth president, then you may be thinking: "What about the Emancipation Proclamation?"

The Emancipation Proclamation was an executive order Lincoln signed on September 22, 1862, that freed all the slaves in the *Confederacy* effective January 1, 1863. It *didn't* free the slaves in the states of Missouri, Kentucky, Maryland, and Delaware, though.

You may be reading this wondering, "Well, what was that all about then?"

Well, it was honestly quite a cynical - and you could say badass - political move by Lincoln. Remember that things weren't going well for the Union on the battlefield in 1862, and the Republicans lost the House of Representatives that year as well. Lincoln had to shake things up to keep hope in the war effort, and he also had to do something to hurt the morale of the Confederacy. After much consideration and talk with his closest advisors, the Emancipation Proclamation seemed to be the perfect ploy to score some political points.

The abolitionists in the Northeast would be pleased by the effort and at the same time, newly freed Blacks who made their way north could be enlisted in Union Army regiments. On the other side, the wave of Black migrants leaving the South would do great damage to the Confederate economy. All the able-bodied White males in the South were fighting the war, leaving their slaves to work the fields. Once the Emancipation Proclamation was ordered, there was nobody to keep them from leaving, and afterwards, there was no one to work the farms and plantations.

Finally, the slave states that remained in the Union were allowed to keep their slaves, at least for the remainder of the war, which kept them firmly in the Union camp.

So, yes - Lincoln did free the slaves, sort of. The reason he did it, though, was more about winning the war and less about the institution of slavery. Some people would say that the cynical move diminishes Lincoln's standing as a humanitarian, while others would say that it just shows how much of a badass politician and leader he was.

After all, many historians claim that the Emancipation Proclamation played a major role in the Union's victory.

LINCOLN QUOTES ON SLAVERY

- "Whenever I hear anyone arguing for slavery, I feel a strong impulse to see it tried on him personally."

- "Slavery is founded on the selfishness of man's nature - opposition to it on his love of justice. These principles are in eternal antagonism; and when brought into collision so fiercely as slavery extension brings them, shocks and throes and convulsions must ceaselessly follow." – Abraham Lincoln on a speech he delivered on October 16, 1854 about the repeal of the Missouri Compromise.

- "In giving freedom to the slave, we assure freedom to the free - honorable alike in what we give and what we preserve. We shall nobly save, or meanly lose, the last best hope of earth." – Lincoln's annual message to Congress on December 1, 1862.

- "In giving freedom to the slave, we assure freedom to the free."

- "As I would not be a slave, so I would not be a master. This expresses my idea of democracy."

CHAPTER 23

"FOUR SCORE AND SEVEN YEARS AGO"

We know that Abraham Lincoln was a badass public speaker and that his speaking abilities were one of the primary reasons for his success. Throughout Lincoln's much too short life he made plenty of speeches, gave several addresses, and was involved in several notable debates, but if you had to identify Lincoln's most badass speech, most will say it was the "Gettysburg Address."

You have no doubt heard the introduction to speech at least once in your life: "Four score and seven years ago our fathers brought forth on this continent, a new nation, conceived in Liberty, and dedicated to the proposition that all men are created equal."

But what made the Gettysburg Address so badass?

Lincoln delivered the Gettysburg Address on November 19, 1863, at the National Cemetery in Gettysburg, Pennsylvania, just four months after the Union defeated the Confederacy on the same grounds. At only 271 words, the speech commemorating the men who died in the battle was concise and to the point, much like Lincoln.

It was important because it proved to be a morale boost for the North and it later became one of the most important speeches in American history.

The North had been losing battle after battle until Gettysburg, and although the Union victory at Gettysburg maybe wasn't the true turning point of the war, it was the beginning of the turning point.

And Lincoln was there, in the middle of a throng of supporters, to let Americans know that as bad as things were, they would get better and that those who sacrificed everything in the struggle would never be forgotten.

Lincoln Quotes about the US Constitution

- "We the people are the rightful masters of both Congress and the courts, not to overthrow the Constitution but to overthrow the men who pervert the Constitution."

- "Don't interfere with anything in the Constitution. That must be maintained, for it is the only safeguard of our liberties."

- "I never did ask more, nor ever was willing to accept less, than for all the States, and the people thereof, to take and hold their places, and their rights, in the Union, under the Constitution of the United States. For this alone have I felt authorized to struggle; and I seek neither more nor less now."

- "Without the Constitution and the Union, we could not have attained the result; but even these, are not the primary cause of our great prosperity. There is something back of these, entwining itself more closely about the human heart."

- "Continue to execute all the express provisions of our national Constitution, and the Union will endure forever - it being impossible to destroy it, except by some action not provided for in the instrument itself." – From Lincoln's first inaugural address on March 4, 1861.

CHAPTER 24

FIGHTING THE COPPERHEADS

Many people think that once Lincoln was elected and the war began, it was pretty easy for him politically. It makes sense, right? What real opposition was there to Lincoln and his ideas in the North once the war began? Well, since you've probably read the book to this point, then you know that it wasn't necessarily so easy. The Democrats took control of the House of Representatives in 1862, which put a check on some of what Lincoln did.

But most of the Democrats in the North were known as "War Democrats"; they believed in fighting the war. There was, though, a considerable faction of Democrats known as the "Copperheads." The Copperheads were a coalition of slave-owning border Democrats, former Southerners who had moved north and urban German and Irish immigrants who had no desire to fight in a war that they believed was being waged on behalf of Blacks.

The Copperheads ran several newspapers and organized in the streets. Copperhead street activity was so well-planned and intense that it even led to riots in New York City from

July 13-16, 1863 over the draft. Needless to say, Lincoln and the Republicans had a real problem with the Copperheads.

When the Union forces lost battles, the Copperheads gained new followers, and the institution of the draft in 1863 also helped to swell their ranks in urban areas. Some thought that the Copperheads posed a real threat to Lincoln's chance of re-election in 1864; they stated they would immediately end the war if their candidate was elected.

There wasn't much Lincoln could do to fight the Copperheads other than to win on the battlefield, which he began to do after he made General Grant his man. The Democrats themselves then sabotaged any chances they had of winning when they shut the Copperheads out of their convention and nominated one of the generals Lincoln had fired, George McClellan. Since McClellan was a War Democrat, it left the voters with no real difference in presidential choices.

The people decided to stay with Honest Abe until the end of the war.

LINCOLN QUOTES ABOUT POLITICS

- "The shepherd drives the wolf from the sheep's for which the sheep thanks the shepherd as his liberator, while the wolf denounces him for the same act as the destroyer of liberty. Plainly, the sheep and the wolf are not agreed upon a definition of liberty." – Address in Baltimore, Maryland on April 18, 1864.

- "Honest statesmanship is the wise employment of individual meanness for the public good."

- "A statesman is he who thinks in the future generations, and a politician is he who thinks in the upcoming elections."

- "Politicians are a set of men who have interests aside from the interests of the people and who, to say the most of them, are, taken as a mass, at least one long step removed from honest men." – Lincoln in front of the Illinois State Assembly on January 11, 1837.

- "My politics are short and sweet, like the old woman's dance."

CHAPTER 25

"LET US NOT JUDGE, THAT YE BE NOT JUDGED"

If the Gettysburg Address was the most badass speech Lincoln gave during his presidency, his second inaugural address was his most important and second in terms of being badass.

After easily winning his second term in 1864, Lincoln had a war to win. Although there was still a lot of war left to be fought and the Confederate forces weren't going away quietly, things were certainly moving in the right direction for Lincoln, Grant, and the Union when the president gave his second inaugural address on March 4, 1865.

The tone and the content of the speech were extremely important and very much indicative of Lincoln's character. Many Republicans wanted Lincoln to take a forceful tone that put the South "in its place," but he decided to go another route.

Drawing heavily on his upbringing and knowledge of scripture—the title of this chapter is a line from the speech Lincoln took from Mathew 7:1 - Lincoln infused plenty of Bible verses in his speech that was heavy on the divine, his ability to forgive, and the unseen hand that drives all of us through life. The address was truly on the esoteric level, so much so that even today many scholars argue over its true meaning.

If you read the speech, you will realize how complex, yet simple it is, just like Lincoln himself. Although we may not be able to understand God entirely, we know enough to know what is right and what is wrong. And in the end, despite differences of opinions, we should always welcome back members of our families into the fold even after they've done wrong.

Now that's a pretty badass way of looking at the world!

Lincoln Quotes about God, Religion, and Spirituality

- "The Almighty has his own purposes. 'Woe unto the world because of offenses! For it must needs be that offenses come; but woe to that man by whom the offense cometh.'" – From Lincoln's second inaugural address.

- "And having thus chosen our course, without guile, and with pure purpose, let us renew our trust in God, and go forward without fear, and with manly hearts."

- "With malice toward none; with charity for all; with firmness in the right, as God gives us to see the right, let us strive on to finish the work we are in; to bind up the nation's wounds; to care for him who shall have borne the battle, and for his widow, and his orphan—to do all which may achieve and cherish a just and lasting peace among ourselves, and with all nations." – Closing remarks from Lincoln's second inaugural address.

- "It will not do to investigate the subject of religion too closely, as it is apt to lead to infidelity."

- "Now, at the end of three years struggle the nation's condition is not what either party, or any man devised, or expected. God alone can claim it."

CHAPTER 26

WINNING THE WAR

By late 1864, it was apparent to everyone that the Union would win the war. General Sherman ravaged Georgia in his infamous march to the sea, the Confederate capital of Richmond had fallen, and General Lee lost his last chance to force the Union to the negotiating table at the Battle of Five Forks on April 1, 1865.

The final battle took place at Appomattox Court House in Virginia on April 9, 1865. It was there that General Lee surrendered his command and the Confederacy was officially finished.

For Lincoln, it was a major relief, but it was also a major let down in some ways. Of course, Lincoln was glad that the war was over, but he also knew that the change of perspective would bring whole new challenges and stresses. Lincoln had to change the entire way he looked at and dealt with the country overnight.

Think about it: Lincoln was a war-time president pretty much from the time he was inaugurated until a few months into his second term. Everything he did in his first term had to do directly with winning the war. Lincoln wasn't afraid to suspend civil liberties and do things with a bit of a dictatorial element, and the people were fine with him doing so, but once the war ended, he needed to quickly change gears.

In April 1865, once he had won the war, Lincoln suddenly had to become a peacetime president.

There were so many things that Honest Abe had to deal with in early 1865, from reviving the American economy to figuring out what to do with the newly freed slaves, and perhaps most importantly, what to do with the vanquished Confederates.

Yes, Lincoln had to face many problems in 1865, but as a truly badass president, he had the background to get things done.

Lincoln Quotes about Victory and Winning

- "Beware of rashness, but with energy and sleepless vigilance go forward and give us victories."

- "Force is all conquering, but its victories are short lived."

- "If you would win a man to your cause, first convince him that you are his sincere friend." – Lincoln to the Springfield Washington Temperance Society on February 22, 1842.

- "I am not bound to win, but I am bound to be true. I am not bound to succeed, but I am bound to live up to what light I have."

- "The one victory we can ever call complete will be that one which proclaims that there is not one slave or one drunkard on the face of God's green earth."

CHAPTER 27

MERCY FOR THE VANQUISHED?

So what separates a leader like Abraham Lincoln from one like Joseph Stalin, making him a true badass? Well, Lincoln and Stalin obviously had many differences, but if you boiled it down to one word, it would be mercy. Yes, mercy, the quality that includes forgiveness, humility, and a desire to leave the past in the past. The most adored badass leaders throughout history are all known for their mercy, while those leaders who are remembered as tyrants consistently showed a lack of mercy throughout their lives.

We've seen how Lincoln was the type of guy who didn't hold grudges and always looked to the future instead of dwelling on the past, which was best demonstrated even before the Civil War had ended.

As the war was winding down, Lincoln and the Republicans knew that it would be a major effort to graft the rebellious Southern states back into the Union, and it immediately became clear that he sat in the middle of a very contentious fight.

On the one side—represented by the Democrats in the North and some Republicans—were those who believed that the

Southern states should be readmitted to the Union as painlessly as possible. They believed that all should be forgiven with little to no penalties for the rebels.

On the other side, was what was known as the "Radical Republicans." They wanted to impose harsh military rule on the South, disenfranchise nearly all Southerners, redistribute land owned by southern Whites to former slaves, and enfranchise their former slaves, thereby creating a new political and social system in the South.

Once again, Lincoln found himself walking a tight rope between the factions. He essentially ended up siding with the moderate Republicans and Democrats. Once when he was asked what should be done with the vanquished Southerners, he replied, "Let'em up easy."

It was a tough position for Lincoln to take, and even today some fault him for it, but it's important to remember that he believed the country would only heal through mercy.

Lincoln Quotes on
Mercy and Forgiveness

- "The damnest scoundrel that ever lived, but in the infinite mercy of Providence... also the damnest fool."

- "Thus let bygones be bygones. Let past differences, as nothing be." – From Lincoln's December 10, 1856 speech at the Republican Party banquet in Chicago, Illinois.

- "Hypocrite: The man who murdered his parents, and then pleaded for mercy on the grounds that he was an orphan."

- "Must I shoot a simple-minded soldier boy who deserts, while I must not touch a hair of the wily agitator who induces him to desert? I think that in such a case to silence the agitator and save the boy is not only constitutional but withal a great mercy."

- "But let the past as nothing be. For the future my view is that the fight must go on."

CHAPTER 28

THE FATHER OF A NEW AMERICA

By the time Lincoln made his fateful visit to the Ford Theater on April 14, 1865, he had built a pretty badass resume for himself. Lincoln had survived the American frontier, fought in an Indian war, built a successful law practice, served his community in the state and US Congress, and finally was elected as the nation's sixteenth president amid America's greatest conflict.

And he won the conflict!

Lincoln's victory in the Civil War assured that he'd be remembered not only as the father of a new political party but in some ways as the father of a new America. George Washington will forever rightfully be remembered as *the* father of America, but Lincoln's presidency represents the birth of something new.

After Lincoln, the Republican Party was the dominant party for the remainder of the century and continued to be one of the two major political parties in the United States.

Most importantly, Lincoln's presidency marked the end of slavery in the United States and the slow but steady move towards political racial equality. Lincoln may not have believed in racial equality, but his presidency paved the way for the Thirteenth, Fourteenth, and Fifteenth Amendments of the United States Constitution. Due to his anti-slavery advocacy, millions of Black Americans were enfranchised, with many viewing him as their favorite president.

It was a tough road for Lincoln from the beginning, but on the night that he went to the Ford Theater, he was riding high with optimism. The North overwhelmingly loved him, and he believed that a majority of the South would come around to accept him.

Because of all this, historians often view Lincoln's presidency, especially after the Civil War ended, as the beginning of a new era in American government, politics, and history. Many of the old ideas were strongly modified, if not thrown out altogether, and in their place were a new set of laws and standards that set the tone for how America is understood today.

Not to mention, Lincoln certainly brought a different style to the Whitehouse as well!

Gone were the powdered wigs and smooth faces of the original founding fathers. Lincoln favored a cropped haircut and a top hat. Perhaps most importantly, Lincoln made the goatee cool!

For all of these reasons, Abraham Lincoln is today considered among *the* Founding Fathers. He may not have been of the original generation of 17776, but he carried their spirit and beliefs forward for a new generation and a new America, and for that, he is often considered among the Founding Fathers of the United States.

LINCOLN QUOTES ABOUT ECONOMICS

- "Teach economy. That is one of the first and highest virtues. It begins with saving money."

- "The money power preys on the nation in times of peace, and conspires against it in times of adversity. It is more despotic than monarchy, more insolent than autocracy, more selfish than bureaucracy. It denounces, as public enemies, all who question its methods or throw light upon its crimes."

- "My old father used to have a saying: If you make a bad bargain, hug it all the tighter."

- "I don't believe in a law to prevent a man from getting rich; it would do more harm than good. So while we do not propose any war upon capital, we do wish to allow the humblest man an equal chance to get rich with everybody else." – From a speech Lincoln delivered in New Haven, Connecticut on March 6, 1860, as he began his campaign for the presidency.

- "Let not him who is houseless pull down the house of another, but let him work diligently to build one for himself, thus by example assuring that his own shall be safe from violence."

CHAPTER 29

EVEN A BADASS CAN'T STOP AN ASSASSIN'S BULLETS

When you've led an important, influential, and badass life to the extent that Abraham Lincoln did, you're bound to make a few enemies. Lincoln always knew that there was a sizable segment of the population who didn't like him and that more than a few people wanted him dead. Lincoln had already lived through the plot to assassinate him in Baltimore, but as the war ended, it looked like such dangers had passed.

Southerners were defeated and feeling demoralized, but their leaders Jefferson Davis and General Lee accepted the loss, so most of them did as well.

It also helped that Lincoln publicly took the stance of reconciliation with the South. The average Southerner had no love for Lincoln, to put it mildly, but most influential Southerners also saw that Lincoln was far better than the alternatives. Southern land-owners and elites argued that although Lincoln may have been a Republican and the reason for their temporary loss of fortunes, he was not a *Radical* Republican.

Slavery was over, but as long as Lincoln was at the helm, the planter class would get its rights back and keep its possessions.

But that still wasn't enough to still the hatred of some in the South.

So, after the war was over, Lincoln carried on with his work and made public appearances to show *all* Americans that life was returning to normal, sort of. Of course, slavery was over and other details about the South's surrender would have to be worked out, but in the meantime, Lincoln needed to continue to project his image of strength.

Unfortunately, it was that projection of strength and Lincoln's badass nature that eventually led to his demise.

Trying to Build a New America

The evening of April 14, 1865, began as a relatively normal night for President Lincoln. It wasn't just like any other night, though. The war had just ended and the streets of Washington were filled with a combination of euphoria, relief, and a little tension. Most people were truly happy that the war was over, but Washington sits right across the river from Virginia and is bordered on its other three sides by the former slave state of Maryland, which was also a hotbed of pro-Confederate sympathizers.

Sympathizers like Maryland-born actor John Wilkes Booth.

Booth was not to be a lone wolf assassin, though. He conspired with several other men to assassinate Vice President Andrew Johnson and members of the cabinet along with the president.

Lincoln was said to have had a dream of his assassination before it happened, but like a true badass, he didn't let that stop him from carrying out his duties. Lincoln continued to make public appearances and on the night of April 14, he and his wife met Major Harry Rathbone and his fiancé Clara Harris to watch a production of the play *Our American Cousin* at the Ford Theater in a private box.

The rest of the story is one of the greatest tragedies in American history.

After Booth crept into Lincoln's private box and shot him in the head, the president only had hours to live. Most people would have immediately died, but Lincoln even briefly regained consciousness before finally losing his last battle.

Witnesses claim that Lincoln died relatively peacefully considering the situation, a true testament to his badass nature.

LINCOLN QUOTES ABOUT LIFE, DEATH, AND THE FUTURE

- "If they do kill me, I shall never die another death."

- "I happen temporarily to occupy this big White House. I am living witness that any one of your children may look to come here as my father's child has." – Lincoln's speech to the 166th Ohio Regiment of the Union Army on August 22, 1864.

- "We know nothing of what will happen in future, but by the analogy of experience."

- "I don't know who my grandfather was; I am much more concerned to know what his grandson will be."

- "The best thing about the future is that it comes one day at a time."

CHAPTER 30

ONE OF THE MOST BADASS LEGACIES OF ALL AMERICAN PRESIDENTS

Likeness on coin currency - check!

Likeness on paper currency - check!

Likeness on a national monument - check and check!

Positive portrayal in countless television shows and movies, including in a *Star Trek* episode and a vampire move - check!

When it comes to American presidents, few others have been able to walk the fine line between stately hero and pop culture icon better than Abraham Lincoln, which alone make him a true badass. We've already talked a bit about Abraham Lincoln's legacy in terms of how he changed the country and essentially became the second founding father, but his legacy is with Americans every day in many ways that many are not even aware of.

Increasing Popularity

Immediately after he was assassinated, Abraham Lincoln became an American martyr and a hero in the North. He was much less popular in the South, but once Reconstruction was over and many of the Confederate veterans had died, his reputation was rehabilitated in the eyes of many Southerners. By the early 1900s, Lincoln had become so popular throughout the country that the United States Treasury Department decided to put Lincoln's likeness on the one-cent coin in 1909.

Now, you might be thinking, "It's just a penny, they aren't worth much." The truth is that Lincoln was the first president to have his likeness on a coin. If you have one of those pennies that were minted through 1958 — often called "wheat pennies" due to the wheat design on their back-side — they are worth at least twice their face value, often much more if they display key dates.

As cool as that is, Lincoln's likeness was then placed on the $5 Federal Reserve Note in 1914, which later became the $5 bill.

As badass as it is to have your likeness on two values of currency, it's even more badass to be on two national monuments.

Lincoln's nineteen-foot-tall, seated statue is the centerpiece of the Lincoln Memorial in Washington, DC, which was finished in 1922. The Memorial has been the site of scenes in TV shows and movies and has served as the backdrop for countless political speeches and protests.

Just three years after the Lincoln Memorial was complete, Lincoln's likeness went up on another American monument — Mount Rushmore. Lincoln's face, alongside presidents Washington, Jefferson, and Theodore Roosevelt, looks from the South Dakota Mountain across the Black Hills and America as if to say that he will forever be here to support Americans. Very few American presidents have one national monument, but Lincoln is among only three (with Washington and Jefferson) to be on two.

The legacy of Lincoln has truly extended all aspects of American culture, even our pop culture. Abraham Lincoln once helped Captain Kirk in a *Star Trek* episode titled "The Savage Curtain," and he killed quite a few vampires in the 2010 novel and 2012 film *Abraham Lincoln: Vampire Hunter*, which may seem like a strange turn for such a serious historical personality. But if you think about it for a minute, it's not so strange after all. The tall, lanky Lincoln, with his goatee and top hat, has an appearance that is perfect for fiction and in some ways seems otherworldly.

But the truth is that if Lincoln were here today, he'd probably have a good laugh about it. We know from his writings that he had a good sense of humor and we also know from history that all true badasses are not above a little self-effacing humor.

Perhaps that's the legacy that we'll have of Abraham Lincoln for generations to come. He was a rough and tough politician who wasn't afraid to get a little dirty, but he had ideals on which he wouldn't compromise. He was loyal to his friends and family and tried to see the good in everyone, including his enemies. For good or bad, those are often the ideals to which most people in the United States aspire. Because of Lincoln, they all have an example to follow.

LINCOLN QUOTES ABOUT LOYALTY AND LOVE

- "A man may be loyal to his government and yet oppose the particular principles and methods of administration."

- "The worst thing you can do for those you love is the things they could and should do themselves."

- "Love is the chain whereby to bind a child to its parents."

- "I remember my mother's prayers and they have always followed me. They have clung to me all my life."

- "It is my pleasure that my children are free and happy, and unrestrained by parental tyranny. Love is the chain whereby to bind a child to its parents."

CONCLUSION

American history is full of many men and women who were true badasses. Perhaps one of the biggest factors that have set the prototypical American badass apart from badasses in other parts of the world and from other times was the expanse of the American frontier and the challenges that were presented to anyone who chose to live in it.

Of course, we know about badass lawmen, outlaws, and Indians who made their names on the American frontier, but the sixteenth president, Abraham Lincoln, also cut his teeth and sharpened his knife in the wild woods of what was at the time the American west.

And that is where the story begins of Lincoln's badass life and what set him apart from many of the presidents before and after him. Lincoln wasn't born with a silver spoon in his mouth but instead had to earn - and sometimes fight - for everything he had in life. Lincoln lived the life of a frontiersman, merchant, and lawyer before realizing that he had more than a knack for politics.

Lincoln quickly proved to all who knew him that he had the intelligence to be a statesman, even though other than his height, he just didn't look like a statesman. Many at the time thought Lincoln look a little on the weird side and that he, therefore, had no credible chance of doing much in politics.

Then they heard him speak!

If Lincoln had a superpower, it was his superb speaking skills and his ability to persuade others to join his side. With a charisma that couldn't be quantified and a sly wit to go along with it, Lincoln became famous for his speeches and debates that he delivered first across his home state of Illinois, and then across the United States on his way to the presidency.

And they were no ordinary times when Lincoln became president.

Lincoln took the reins of a new political party to lead the nation at its lowest point when it fractured into two, warring nations. With the evil and antiquated institution of slavery being the driving force for the war, Lincoln rallied the nation and the troops to move forward and fight for what was right. The country fought on, the Union won the war, and the nation eventually came back together.

But unfortunately, as much of a badass as Lincoln was, he didn't live to see the new America he helped build.

As a final testament to Lincoln's influence and badass nature, though, symbols of his life and presidency are everywhere in the United States. After Washington, Lincoln is arguably the best known and most popular president, and possibly the most relatable for a majority of the population.

For all of these reasons, Abraham Lincoln is rightfully considered among the most badass of all American presidents.

DON'T FORGET YOUR FREE BOOKS

MORE BOOKS BY BILL O'NEILL

I hope you enjoyed this book and learned something new.

Please feel free to check out some of my previous books on Amazon.

Made in United States
North Haven, CT
11 December 2022

28489651R00075